THE ART OF
CHINESE
FLOWER
ARRANGEMENT

中国插花

THE ART OF
CHINESE
中国插花 FLOWER
ARRANGEMENT

By Cai Zhongjuan
Translated by Zhao Gang and Du Zhendong

Better Link Press

On page 1

Fig. 1   Lines are the backbones of Chinese flower arrangement. Different lines produce different visual effects on the viewers. We can use various line flowers to achieve this target.

On pages 2 and 3
Fig. 2   *Uniquely Charming*
Arrangement: Chinese pagoda tree, Chinese flowering crabapple, common goldenrod herb, Chinese St. John's wort fruit, chamomile
Vessel: Pottery pot
Artist: Cai Zhongjuan

This is a very traditional Chinese work. Its traditionalism is mirrored in the selection of the vessel, stand, flowers, and composition. In this work, the Chinese pagoda tree blots out the sky and the sun. It looks uniquely powerful, showing originality in design.

On page 6
Fig. 3   *Wind Coming from the East*
Arrangement: Cymbidium, styrax dasyanthus, chamomile, white lace flower, Chinese date
Vessel: Pottery pot
Artist: Cai Zhongjuan

With seven dark blue and light-blue folding fans and several powerfully curly Chinese date branches, this modern work is rich in Chinese flavor. The folding fans are the key components of this work, implying that the wind comes from alongside.

This book is edited and designed by the Editorial Committee of *Cultural China* series

Text: Cai Zhongjuan
Works: Cai Zhongjuan, Ding Wenlin, Liang Shengfang, Wang Luchang, Xie Ming, Yuan Naifu, Chen Hao, Chen Juan, Xu Guodong, Jiang Zhiling, Liu Xin, Chen Jingyi
Illustrations: Gao Hua
Photographs: Li Fangming, Yuan Naifu, Xin Dingcheng, etc., Quanjing

Translation: Zhao Gang, Du Zhendong
Cover Design: Wang Wei
Interior Design: Li Jing, Hu Bin (Yuan Yinchang Design Studio)

Copy Editor: Susan Luu Xiang
Editors: Wu Yuezhou, Cao Yue
Editorial Director: Zhang Yicong

Senior Consultants: Sun Yong, Wu Ying, Yang Xinci
Managing Director and Publisher: Wang Youbu

ISBN: 978-1-60220-026-5

Address any comments about *The Art of Chinese Flower Arrangement* to:

Better Link Press
99 Park Ave
New York, NY 10016
USA

or

Shanghai Press and Publishing Development Company, Ltd.
F 7 Donghu Road, Shanghai, China (200031)
Email: comments_betterlinkpress@hotmail.com

Printed in China by Shenzhen Donnelley Printing Co., Ltd.
1   3   5   7   9   10   8   6   4   2

CONTENTS

CONTENTS

Fig. 4 *Majestic and Spirited*
Arrangement: Pleomele, white bark pine,
lily, chamomile, king protea,
common goldenrod herb, sawara cypress,
box, Chinese pink, gmelin's sea lavender herb
Vessel: Pottery vase
Artist: Cai Zhongjuan

Chinese vase flowers can also be plump and luxurious. Such a work often consists of
gorgeous flowers in balanced composition. It is mostly placed in halls for appreciation.
In ancient time, ten kinds of flowers were often used in arranging such a work,
symbolizing perfection in every way. This work embodies modern Chinese flower
arrangement. It uses ten kinds of flowers, most of which are herbaceous plants. Plump
in form and flamboyant in color, it creates a fine embellishing effect.

Preface

Three things, simple but overwhelmingly strong, have governed my life: the love for the art of Chinese flower arrangement, the devotion to its growth, and the mission to carry it forward.

I was immediately attracted by its beauty when I was first introduced to the art of Chinese flower arrangement in Shanghai as a young landscaping designer. Flowers were beautiful, but those that were artistically treated were even more so, as they offered the flower arranger and the viewer sensory, as well as spiritual enjoyment. How nice it was for me to take up such a job!

The art of flower arrangement is an epitome of earth art, which is the focus of landscaping. My work as a landscape designer and my personal love for flowers pushed me headlong into the field of flower arrangement. I virtually devoted all my spare time at work and then my retirement years to it, arranging flowers myself, writing books and giving lectures on it, organizing flower arrangement associations, and setting up schools for flower arrangement. Fifty years have passed in a wink of an eye, during which I have gradually mastered the art of flower arrangement. The more I know it, the more I love it, and the more persistent I have become with it.

Chinese flower arrangement as an art is time-honored and profound. The primitive form of flower arrangement appeared in China as early as three thousand years ago, rendering China the birthplace of oriental flower arrangement. Since time immemorial, it has given the country the appreciation for the beauty of life and spiritual nourishment. The blending of Chinese floriculture, painting culture, poetic culture, and gardening culture into flower arrangement in later times has finally rendered this form of art a fine traditional Chinese culture.

This book, which intends to introduce to lovers of flower arrangement the historical evolution, styles and characteristics, and techniques of the art of Chinese flower arrangement, aims at helping the readers understand and learn Chinese flower arrangement.

At the completion of this book, I would like to express my heartfelt thanks to those who have provided generous help and support. They are the Shanghai Flower Art and Arrangement Association, the Municipal Government of Changyi City in Shandong Province, the Naifu School of Flower Arrangement in Jinan in Shandong Province, and *Today Flower Arrangement Magazine* in South Korea.

Cai Zhongjuan

CHAPTER ONE
A Brief History

Flower arrangement as a cultural activity has enjoyed a history of at least two to three thousand years in the West and the East. It is a unique decorative art with cultural connotations based on the artistic treatment of clipped garden plants.

Unlike graphic art, such as calligraphy and painting, flower arrangement is three-dimensional. However, it is also different from other forms of three-dimensional art, such as sculpture and architecture, in that it is a work of art with life.

The art of flower arrangement in China is time-honored and profound. With a history of over 3,000 years, it is a major component part of Chinese floriculture.

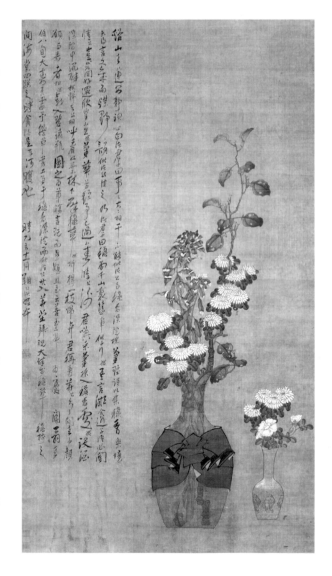

On facing page
Fig. 5 *Flowers and Antique*
Ink and color on silk
Height 127.4 cm × Width 63.3 cm
Palace Museum, Taibei

In this painting is a collection of flower arrangement works in the early Qing Dynasty (1644–1911), which consists of six vase and pot flowers. The floral vessels include bronze goblets, blue-and-white porcelain vases, underglaze blue and underglaze red tube, and cloisonné vases. They are arranged in a scalene triangle, with big vessels interspersed with small ones and tall vessels with low ones. The whole work is hierarchical and varied in form. Equipped with exquisite stands, it is highly ornamental.

Fig. 6 *A Scroll Painting of Vase Flowers*
Chen Hongshou (1598–1652, Ming Dynasty)
Ink and color on silk
Height 175 cm × Width 98.5 cm
British Museum

This work is a combined type of flower arrangement, consisting of chrysanthemums, Chinese roses, and painted euphorbia, etc. The main vase is tall with a handkerchief tied in the middle to show steadiness. The supplementary vase is small, and the flowers in it coordinate with those in the main vase.

1. The Budding Period: Early Zhou Dynasty to the Spring and Autumn and Warring States Periods (11–3 BC)

According to ancient books, such as *The Book of Songs* (*Shi Jing*) and *Elegies of the South* (*Chu Ci*), Chinese people at that time used clipped flowers, plants, and tree branches either as sacrifices to their ancestors or gods, or as headwear or ornaments hanging at the waist, or as gifts to their friends at the time of departure, or as decorations in their houses or boats. This shows that the primitive form of flower arrangement has emerged at that time.

According to a poem in *The Book of Songs*, when young men and women fell in love during a spring outing and pledged to marry, they would exchange branches of Chinese herbaceous peony at the time of departure to express their affection for each other.

Another poem in *The Book of Songs* says: "A fair maiden I'm deeply in love with meets me at the corner wall. She gives me a rare reed. It's lovely not because it is rare, but because it is a gift from my love."

Qu Yuan (340–278 BC), a well-known poet in the State of Chu, wrote in *The Lament* (*Li Sao*): "I used waternut leaves to make my coat and lotus flowers to make my skirt. It does not matter that nobody understands me. What I care for is only that my sentiments remain true and fragrant."

He wrote in another poem about a goddess who decorated a dragon boat with flowers to greet her beloved husband: "The Goddess of the Xiang River went to the Dongting Lake in a dragon boat. She decorated the helm with climbing figs, the tabernacle with aromatic grass, the banners with eupatorium fortune, and the oars with calami. She also gave the serving maids aromatic flowers she picked on the isle."

The above citations show that even in the initial stage of modern civilization, flowers were closely related to people's life. They bestowed flowers with specific meanings and expressed their feelings with them. Flowers have thus become a symbol of culture.

2. The Initial Development Period: Qin and Han Dynasties (221 BC–220 AD)

The feudal Qin and Han dynasties witnessed great socioeconomic development, which, in turn, pushed the development of culture and art. As a result, flower arrangement gradually took shape as an art form. In the mural painted along the passage of an East Han tomb in Wangdu in northern Hebei Province, there is a round pottery pot, in which are six small red flowers, placed on a square stand. This shows that people at that time paid particular attention to the form of flower arrangement. The flower pot was placed on the stand to add to the aesthetic taste.

3. The Formation Period: Northern and Southern Dynasties (420–589)

As was recorded in the *History of Southern Dynasties* (*Nan Shi*) authored by Li Yanshou in the Tang Dynasty (618–907), Zimao, the seventh son of Xiao Ze (440–493), an emperor of the Qi Dynasty (479–502), during the Northern and Southern Dynasties asked the monks to pray for his dying mother when he was seven. When someone offered lotus flowers to the Buddha, the monks kept the flowers fresh by placing them into a bronze earthen jar, a container large in the middle and small at the mouth used for holding water or wine or for offering flowers to the Buddha. This is evidence that, at the time, flowers were mainly used as offerings in the family hall for worshipping Buddha and that people began to keep the flowers fresh by raising them in water.

As time passed, flower arrangement had become increasingly popular. Besides enjoying flowers outdoors, people arranged them into vases and pots for appreciation at home. Flowers gradually ceased to be just a religious offering, but as works for appreciation as well.

4. The Golden Period: Sui, Tang, and the Five Dynasties (581–960)

During this period, flower arrangement witnessed further development in kind and form (fig. 7). Apart from being used in temples as offerings, it appeared in the royal palaces in various forms, i.e. in vases, baskets, urns, bamboo tubes, etc.

Flower offerings to the Buddha were small in number. In one vase should be arranged only one kind of flower, which, in most cases, was the lotus flower. The whole work was often concisely arranged, consisting of a flower, which was the longest, and two leaves. Flower arrangement in royal palaces or in a home, however, involved more flowers in diversified forms. The major flowers used were peonies,

Fig. 7 Image of Water-Moon Goddess of Mercy in the Tang Dynasty. In the flower pot on the right are arranged blooming flowers and buds. Symmetrical in pattern and thriving, they are typical of pot flowers in the early stage.

orchids, plum blossoms, lotus flowers, peach flowers, and apricot flowers, set off by the leaves of pines, willows, and locust trees. Some flowers were arranged in the form of a triangle, while others extended in all directions, looking ceremonious and luxurious. The length of the flower and the height of the floral vessel were of a golden ratio, either 8:5 or 5:8 (fig. 8).

During this period, flower appreciation was also very popular among common folks. In the mid-Tang period, the fifteenth of each February in the lunar calendar was appointed the Day of Flowers, also known as the Festival of the Flower Goddess, to mark the birthday of all flowers. On that day, the whole city would turn out to appreciate flowers, an event ironically recorded by the Tang poet Du Mu (803–853) in his *Apricot Garden*: "The light rain last night washed away dusts from the flowers. Fine horses entered the apricot garden in good order. Don't blame the falling flowers scattering all about. How many flower viewers do you know wear flowers on their heads?"

In addition, people also associated flowers with human traits, which was a breakthrough in the study of flower arrangement. Therefore, in choosing flowers for arrangement, people had become more cautious, as they needed to know well their natural and humanistic qualities.

By then, flower arrangement had been studied as a specialized knowledge. A series of books in this field were published, including *Ode to the Spring Plate* (*Chunpan Fu*) and *Nine Things in Flower Arrangement* (*Hua Jiuxi*) authored respectively by Ouyang Zhan and Luo Qiu in the Tang Dynasty. In *Ode to the Spring Plate*, Ouyang Zhan carefully described how people had used

Fig. 8 Banner painting in the Tang Dynasty. In this painting, the Bodhisattva holds a vase of lotus flowers in her hands. This pattern of flower arrangement, small and upright, is the prototype of the Free-Style arrangement favored by monks and men of letters.

the plate as the soil, and flowers, branches, and grasses as the materials to produce lively scenes of spring. This shows that Miniascape-Style Flower Arrangement had appeared in this period. In *Nine Things in Flower Arrangement*, the author discussed the tools for flower arrangement, such as the container, scissors, and flower stand. Covering almost all ingredients in flower arrangement, this book is considered as the basis for the future development of flower arrangement.

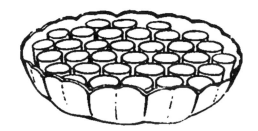

Fig. 9 Plate of Flower Arrangement.

Chinese flower arrangement gradually reached maturity during the Five Dynasties period (907–960). Although flower arrangement at that time was not as popular as in the Sui (581–618) and Tang dynasties due to the chaos caused by the incessant wars, it was invigorated by the participation of men of letters. They resorted to flowers to express their ambitions or drown their sorrows, they were unrestrained in the selection of floral vessels and flowers, and they gave full play to their imagination in flower arrangement, which, finally, brought this form of art to maturity. The most noticeable characteristic of flower arrangement in that period was the focus on the delight of life and the natural interest and charm of the flowers, instead of on extravagance or luxury. The floral vessel was often simple and the flowers chosen were concise in pattern and quietly elegant, mirroring the refined scholastic grace in every aspect. Since many of these men of letters were painters, poets, or writers steeped in aesthetics, it was only too natural that they instill the law of aesthetics into flower arrangement, which, in turn, pushed the development of this art.

The most influential events in the history of Chinese flower arrangement during the Five Dynasties were the creation of the Heavenly Abode of Flowers exhibition and the invention of the Plate of Flower Arrangement tool.

The Heavenly Abode of Flowers exhibition was a grand annual event for flower arrangement in the spring hosted by Li Yu (937–978), the last emperor of the Southern Tang Dynasty (937–975). It was also the earliest flower arrangement exhibition in China. According to records, when the time came for the exhibition, all the beams, ridge poles, pillars, and staircases in the royal palace would be decorated with various kinds of flowers, and hence the name of the Heavenly Abode of Flowers. This shows that, as early as a thousand years ago, exhibitions of flower arrangement had appeared in China, and so had spatial floriculture.

The Plate of Flower Arrangement, invented by Guo Jiangzhou in the Five Dynasties, was a setting tool for flower arrangement. He cast many copper tubes at the bottom of the plate, in which the flowers could be arranged. This invention, which made it easier for flower composition and Miniascape-Style Flower Arrangement, marked a major progress in the techniques of Chinese flower arrangement and was also the rudiment of modern flower arrangement (fig. 9).

5. The Meridian Period: Song Dynasty (960–1279)

After the continuous chaos caused by war, people longed for peace and stability. They took up flower appreciation as something delightful and productive. Thus, it had become a custom for people to view flowers, especially on the Day of Flowers.

In the Song Dynasty, people regarded flower arrangement, incense burning, tea-making, and artistic picture hanging as the four skills of life one must learn to possess in his childhood (fig. 10). Flower arrangement exhibitions at the national and local level gradually gained popularity.

By then, flower arrangement had taken on different looks.

In royal palaces, flowers were arranged either for everyday decoration or for festival celebration. When the Day of Flowers came, the flowers used most often were luxurious and magnificent. Some of the antique vases and pots, which were items of appreciation on their own under normal circumstances, were used to display precious flowers.

The flowers used in royal palaces were often large and colorful with luxuriant foliage and a discreet layout, and were thus known as Palace-Style Flowers. The potted flowers resembled flower arrangement in the West at first glance, but were in fact different under careful examination. The flowers were arranged in a scalene triangle and the branches were zigzag rather than linearly radial. The density between them was just appropriate, bringing out the best in each other. The flowers and foliage might be close, but each of them would stand in comfort and good order. The postures, colors, sizes, and orientations of the flowers were different from each other, giving the viewers a strong sense of rhythm and vitality.

Fig. 10 *Atlas of People's Daily Life*
Anonymous (Northern Song Dynasty, 960–1127)
Ink and color on silk
Height 29 cm × Width 27.8 cm
Palace Museum, Taibei

In the front of this painting is a work of flower arrangement, in the rear is a wall picture, and on the left are burning incenses and boiling tea. The four were known collectively as the "four skills of life," symbolizing a refined lifestyle.

Men of letters in the Song Dynasty paid particular attention to refined elegance in flower arrangement. They often chose materials from fresh and durable flowers and trees, such as pines, cypresses, plums, orchids, bamboo, chrysanthemums, and lotus flowers. A few branches from them would be enough to make the viewers reluctant to depart. Flower arrangement was fashionable among men of letters and scholar-officials of that time as well, as is shown in the poem from the Southern Song (1127–1279) poet Yang Wanli (1127–1206): "The silver vase matches perfectly with the jade-like plum blossoms. Picked from the plum tree in the north, some of them are still in the bud. Living lonely in the hill, I set the table and invite poets for poetry." (fig. 11)

Flower arrangement was even more popular in temples and among common folks during this period. Besides offering flowers to

Fig. 11 *Enjoying the Zither* (section)
Zhao Ji (1082–1135, Northern Song Dynasty)
Ink and color on silk
Height 147.2 cm × Width 51.3 cm
Palace Museum, Beijing

In the Song Dynasty, the materials used for flower arrangement were mainly pine, cypress, bamboo, plum, orchid, sweet osmanthus, camellia, and narcissus that were graceful and refined. They were arranged sparsely to show the author's spiritual pursuits. Such a work emphasized the use of lines and order.

This work in the front of the painting consists of upright and sparsely-spaced flower branches in varied heights and sizes, which are concentrated into a bunch. The floral vessel is clear at the mouth, covered neither by the branches nor the leaves. The whole work is concise and elegantly refined.

Fig. 12 *Flower Basket*
Qian Xuan (c. 1239–1300, Yuan Dynasty)
Ink and color on silk
Height 26.2 cm × Width 30.5 cm
Palace Museum, Taibei

This is a pendent work in a suspended basket in the Yuan Dynasty. The bamboo woven basket is simple and classic, inside which is a pair of big-mouthed celadon vases, which have in them orange sweet osmanthuses and light-yellow sweet osmanthuses respectively. Across the mouths of the vases lies horizontally an osmanthus branch that is shaped like a *ruyi* (scepter border, literally "as you wish") and that bends upward at the end. Unlike previous works of a similar kind, this work presents the charm of asymmetry.

the Buddha, monks also placed flowers in their meditation rooms, on the sutra tables, or simply outdoors. The few branches of flowers were endowed with rich Buddhist mood. Flower arrangement was most common in major cities on the Day of Flowers and during festivals. Flowers were arranged in different forms and styles all year round to match different festival celebrations.

The Idea-Oriented Flower, a new style of vase flower arrangement, appeared in the Song Dynasty, which instilled profound philosophical thinking and doctrines into flower arrangement and focused more on the content than the form of flower arrangement. Taking sparsity as its spirit and thinness as its ideological support, works of this style emphasized the beauty of lines, clarity, elegance, and order. The length of the flower branch and the height of the vase were in the golden ratio, about 1.6 times of the sum of the height of the vase and the diameter of the caliber.

Since flower arrangement was a specialized knowledge in the Song Dynasty, people had conducted more in-depth studies on the character and nature of flowers. Flowers were increasingly personified and were rated based on their categories. For example, Zeng Zao, a Taoist scholar in the early Southern Song Dynasty, rated ten kinds of flowers as friends of different characters, which were orchids, plum blossoms, winter daphne, lotus flowers, grape flowers, winter sweet, chrysanthemums, sweet osmanthuses, Chinese flowering crabapples, and tea millets. Huang Tingjian (1045–1105), a master of literature in the Northern Song Dynasty, treated ten kinds of flowers as guests of different qualities, which included plum blossoms, peach flowers, apricot flowers, narcissi, Chinese herbaceous peonies, lotus flowers, sweet osmanthuses, chrysanthemums, orchids, and tea millets. Other studies on flower species, floral vessels, and vase flower maintenance also witnessed rapid development in the Song Dynasty.

In the Yuan Dynasty (1279–1368), the floriculture grew slowly and even stagnated due to the influence of the overall social environment. People found no time to grow flowers and were not in the mood to appreciate them. Only those scholar-officials who lived in seclusion in mountains could manage to maintain flower arrangement. In adversity, they dispelled their melancholy by arranging the flowers they grew themselves, indulging in self-appreciation. To them, flowers were a means to relieve their loneliness and frustrations and express their subjective thoughts, giving birth to the so-called Mental Image-Oriented Flowers (figs. 12–13). Unlike Idea-Oriented Flowers that were rich in philosophical connotations, Mental Image-Oriented Flowers reflected individual mood and interest. The flowers chosen were mostly symbolic and embodied natural charm, focusing on expressing individual emotions, displaying the beauty of mental images, and presenting the inspirations Chinese men of letters obtained from nature and life.

Fig. 13 *The Harmonious Colors of Spring*
Zhang Zhong (Yuan Dynasty)
Ink and color on paper
Height 99.1 cm × Width 41.1 cm
Palace Museum, Taibei

This vase of peonies was painted by Zhang Zhong in the Yuan Dynasty, consisting of pink, white, and red peonies. The large space between the flowers is taken up by peony leaves. The floral vessel is a refreshing long-neck white vase.

6. The Revival Period: Ming Dynasty (1368–1644)

In the early Ming Dynasty, Zhu Yuanzhang (1328–1398), the first Ming emperor, forbade the building of gardens for flower growing in the royal palace, so flower arrangement was only encouraged on happy or festive occasions. This had rendered this form of art less popular than in the previous dynasties. However, propelled by the agricultural development of that time, flower breeding among common folks saw unprecedented growth, which further popularized flower arrangement as a folk art (figs. 14–15). The temple of the Flower Goddess was built in many places and people rushed to give their offerings there on the Day of Flowers.

During this period, the minds of scholars were emancipated and the

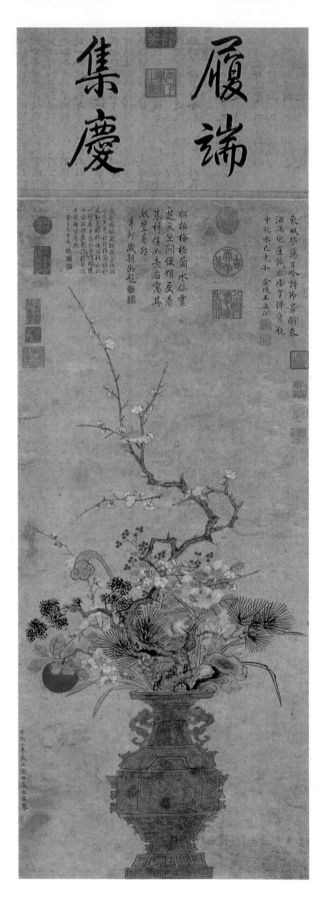

Fig. 14 *Painting for the New Year*
Bian Wenjin (Ming Dynasty)
Ink and color on paper
Height 108 cm × Width 46.1 cm
Palace Museum, Taibei

This work was often placed in the hall during the Ming Dynasty. It consists of ten elements, such as plum blossom, pine, cypress, camellia, orchid, narcissus, *lingzhi* mushroom, sacred bamboo, persimmon, and a *ruyi*, implying perfection in every way. Later, this style of flower arrangement was introduced to Japan and became the earliest ancestor of the *Ikenobo*, the oldest and most important school of Japanese ikebana.

atmosphere of returning to the ancients and of mental cultivation was prevalent. As a result, studies in flower arrangement prospered, giving birth to a series of publications in this field, such as *Three Theories of Vase Flower Arrangement* (*Pinghua Sanshuo*) by the dramatist Gao Lian (c. 1527–1603), *The Trivial of a Hermit* (*Kaopan Yushi*) by the dramatist and writer Tu Long (1543–1605), *On Vase Flower Arrangement* (*Pinghua Pu*) by Zhang Qiande (1577–1643), *History of Vases* (*Ping Shi*) by the writer Yuan Hongdao (1568–1610), and *A Record of Useful Tricks* (*Zhangwu Zhi*) by Wen Zhenheng (1585–1645).

When *History of Vases* came out in 1600, it caused a great sensation in China, facilitating the popularity of flower arrangement of that time. In 1696, the book was translated into Japanese by a Japanese scholar and was published in Japan, exerting a profound influence on Japanese flower arrangement and giving rise to the Hongdao School of flower arrangement in Japan.

Men of letters in the Ming Dynasty were particular not only about the outlook of flower arrangement, but also the connotations it carries. The way the flowers were arranged was often a reflection of the ideals and wishes of the arranger. Although similar to the Idea-Oriented Flower

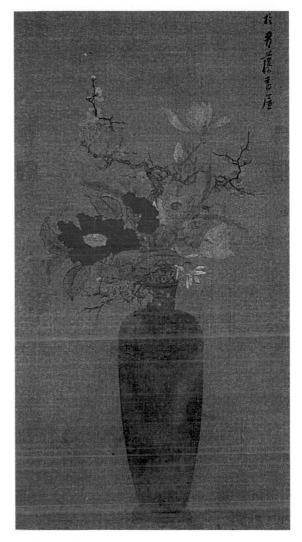

Fig. 15 *New Year's Flowers*
Chen Hongshou (Ming Dynasty)
Ink and color on silk
Height 90.2 cm × Width 41.1 cm
Palace Museum, Taibei

In ancient works of flower arrangement, the ratio between the height of the first main branch and that of the vase was often 8:5 (i.e., the golden ratio) or 5:8. This work was created in the late Ming Dynasty, consisting of such flowers as plum blossom, camellia, magnolia, narcissus, and orchid.

arrangement in the Song Dynasty, flower arrangement in the Ming Dynasty was more concise in form and emphasized the virtues of the flowers used. It is thus known as New Idea-Oriented Flower Arrangement, which not only pursued the classical and complete forms of flower arrangement, but also displayed the beauty of law, personality, and harmony in human society by means of presenting the natural beauty of the flowers. In such works, the viewers could find the arrangers' expectations of the social orders and their philosophies of life, which were not typical of an individual, but of the whole society, including what was ethical, good, and beautiful.

Fig. 16 This was a product in the Ming Dynasty arranged in a flower basket. The flowers used are Chinese roses, lychnis coronata, and smartweeds, etc. The basket is made of vines, dark and strong. The holes enable the viewer to appreciate the flowers inside and above the basket. With graceful flowers bathed in the warmth of the autumn sunshine, the whole work looks distinctive and charming.

Men of letters often arranged flowers loosely to give the viewers a feeling of freshness and elegance (fig. 16). For this purpose, they usually chose branches with few flowers or leaves to achieve beauty of lines and tranquility (see fig. 6 on page 11).

Flower arrangement in the Ming Dynasty mainly took the form of vase flowers. There were two major kinds of vases, known as Golden House and Refined Hut. The former referred to the stately copper vases and cloisonné vases, which were used in such former places as the palace, halls, and temples. The latter referred to graceful and simple small floral vessels made of porcelain, which were used in such elegant places as the study and fast room.

7. The Declining Period: Qing Dynasty (1644–1911)

Flower arrangement was still flourishing in the early Qing Dynasty and it was popular even during the reign of the Empress Dowager (1835–1908) in the late Qing Dynasty. However, after the Opium War, it went into decline along with the political and economic recessions.

In the early Qing Dynasty, flower arrangement in the palace inherited the Idea-Oriented Style of the Ming Dynasty. The floral vessels were gorgeous and the flowers chosen were often bright-colored, such as red and yellow. Flower arrangement among common folks was even more popular. On some festive occasions, the commoners would join with the temples to host flower arrangement exhibitions or contests, attracting quite a lot of attention (fig. 17 and see figs. 18–19 on page 24).

Under the influence of the *penjing* (potted scenery) art, the Miniascape-Style flower arrangement was more prevalent then, including flowers without roots and combination bonsai with roots. Meanwhile, Model-Oriented Flower Arrangement and flower arrangement using vegetables and fruits began to emerge (see fig. 20 on page 25).

Although artistic creation in flower arrangement stagnated in the Qing Dynasty, studies in flower appreciation and theories of flower arrangement were as good as previous dynasties. For example, different kinds of flowers were matched with the names of celebrities in different dynasties and were thus worshipped as flower goddesses. Each of the twelve months of the year was paired with a flower, giving birth to the worshipping of the twelve goddesses of flowers.

Monographs on flower arrangement in the Qing Dynasty included *Feelings Jotted*

Fig. 17 *Bouquet of Auspiciousness*
Lang Shining (Giuseppe Castiglione, Italy, 1688–1766)
Ink and color on silk
Height 173 cm × Width 86.1 cm
Palace Museum, Taibei

This was a Miniascape-Style Flower Arrangement created in the Qing Dynasty. It mainly consists of twin lotus flowers and lotus seed pods, which are supplemented with dasheen leaves and rice ears. The whole work looks graceful and natural, with branches swaying in the wind.

Fig. 19 *The Harmonious Colors of Spring*
Aisin Gioro Mianyi (18th–19th century, Qing Dynasty)
Ink and color on paper
Height 81.7 cm × Width 36 cm
Palace Museum, Taibei

This work was created to celebrate the Spring Festival. The flowers used include plum blossoms, sacred bamboo, Chinese roses, and azaleas. On the floor beside the vase are placed narcissi, lily, persimmons, and a *ruyi*, implying good luck in everything. This style of flower arrangement was popular from the Yuan Dynasty to the Qing Dynasty and was particularly favored among common folks.

Fig. 18 *Beautiful Scenery for the New Year*
Chen Shu (17th–18th century, Qing Dynasty)
Ink and color on silk
Height 96.8 cm × Width 47 cm
Palace Museum, Taibei

Arranged in an urn, this work was created to celebrate the Lantern Festival in the Qing Dynasty. It integrated the aesthetic principles of flower arrangement and the pot-culture method of rooted plants, a technique known as combined pot culture in modern times. The flowers used were plum blossoms, camellias, sacred bamboo, and narcissi, which were set off by mountain rocks. On the floor beside the urn were lily, persimmons, and a *ruyi*, implying auspiciousness.

Fig. 20 *Overflowing with Spring Vigor*
Zou Yigui (1686–1772, Qing Dynasty)
Ink and color on paper
Height 42.2 cm × Width 74.5 cm
Palace Museum, Taibei

This was a *Penjing*-Style Flower Arrangement in the early Qing Dynasty, a style that was started also in this dynasty. This work focuses on portraying a courtyard or rustic view. It is based on small bamboo and palm trees, which are set off by a Taihu rock and the pebbles that cover the surface of the pot.

Down Occasionally (*Xianqing Ouji*) by the drama theoretician and writer Li Yu (1611–1680), *Dream Shadows* (*Youmeng Ying*) by the writer Zhang Chao (1650–?), and *Six Chapters of a Floating Life: the Little Pleasures of Life* (*Fusheng Liuji: Xianqing Jiqu*) by Shen Fu (1763–?).

Due to the incessant wars in the Late Qing period, people lived in great hardship. As a result, flower arrangement as an art gradually went into decline.

In the early 1980s, along with the development of Chinese economy and culture, Chinese flower arrangement ushered in a new phase of development. Flower arrangement associations were organized one after another in several major cities like Beijing, Shanghai, and Guangzhou, which focus on studying the art of flower arrangement, hosting flower arrangement exhibitions, and starting flower arrangement classes. In 2008, Chinese flower arrangement entered the list of state-level non-material cultural heritages. Today, besides thousands and thousands of amateur flower arrangement lovers, there is also a team of flower arrangement experts who have received their job qualification certificates after being trained, examined, and assessed. At the same time, flower arrangement is offered as a major in some institutions of higher learning to train high-level talents in this field. International exchanges in the field of flower arrangement have witnessed vigorous growth and flower arrangement has become a kind of creative industry. All these achievements have never appeared in Chinese history and the new era will bring new life to this time-honored artistic tradition.

Fig. 21 *Refreshing Lotus Fragrance in Summer*
Arrangement: Lotus seed pod, lotus leaf, pond lily, styrax dasyanthus
Vessel: Wooden frame
Artist: Cai Zhongjuan

Arranged in a black picture frame, this work looks exactly like a Chinese painting, the difference being that a painting is one-dimensional while this work is three-dimensional. It makes the viewer feel cool and refreshing as if they were standing on the bank of a lotus pond in a hot summer.

CHAPTER TWO
Styles and Characteristics

China and the ancient Egypt are home to flower arrangement in the East and West, respectively. Due to different geographical locations, cultures, histories, national characteristics, and religious beliefs, the artistic styles in the East and West are poles apart, which is shown in many fields of art, including painting, sculpture, architecture, music, and gardening. Flower arrangement is no exception, as it derives from the same origin as other forms of Chinese art.

Several factors have influenced Chinese flower arrangement, i.e. the ancient Chinese philosophical idea of harmony between man and nature, the ancient Chinese calligraphic and painting art, and the flower arrangement practice of ancient Chinese men of letters. As a result, Chinese flower arrangers follow the way of nature in showcasing life in miniature, emphasize the use of lines to make their works vivid, and strive to display artistic conceptions with the inner beauty of their works. All these factors have helped shape the styles and characteristics of Chinese flower arrangement, which, in brief, are the focus on the beauty of nature, lines, and artistic conceptions, forming a striking contrast with flower arrangement in the West which emphasizes the beauty of manpower, patterns, and ornamentation.

Fig. 22 *The Boundless Vista Is at the Perilous Peak*
Arrangement: Sacred bamboo, anise, chamomile, common goldenrod herb, asparagus myriocladus, bark
Vessel: Imitation porcelain plastic pot
Artist: Cai Zhongjuan

This work portrays a lakeside view. It uses several barks to create jagged mountain peaks that, looking up to heaven, are free and facile. The leaves and fruits of the sacred bamboo in the front or behind the peaks are indispensible because they diversify the hierarchy and colors of this work, form a contrast with the mountain rocks, and make the work vigorous and agile. Beneath the rocks is a cluster of common goldenrod herbs and chamomile that bring out the moisture in the quiet valley. With several simple materials, this work intends to create a complicated natural wonder featuring a boundless vista at the top of the towering peaks.

Fig. 23 *Peonies Swaying in Spring Breezes*
Arrangement: Peony, Chinese flowering crabapple, false spirea, asparagus myriocladus
Vessel: Porcelain vase
Artist: Cai Zhongjuan

The method of asymmetric balance is often adopted in Chinese flower arrangement. The materials are chosen for their natural freshness and vitality, rather than for their species, number, and color. In this work, the peonies symbolize spring and the extending twigs of the false spirea resemble the dancing west wind, constituting a harmonious scene of activity and inertia.

1. Following the Way of Nature

Chinese flower arrangers seek for the harmonious coexistence between man and nature, striving to capture the beautiful scenes of nature in their works.

They display life by imitating nature and treat the flowers most appropriately to integrate the best part of nature into their works. Under their hands, the flowers and leaves look vivid and natural, as if they were the work of nature. The arrangers derive their works from nature, but present them on a higher plane than nature itself.

Asymmetric balance in composition is often pursued, because this is typical of many types of scenery in nature, such as the undulating mountains, winding rivers, trees of various heights, etc. These irregularities bring about endless changes and yet exist in harmony, giving birth to diversified types of memorable works.

The flowers to be used should be fresh and lively, rather than wilted, except for the expression of a special theme. Generally, the branches, leaves, flowers, fruits, and vines of a plant should be used at the same time in a work, and so should the buds, budding blossoms, and full-blown flowers, so as to fully display the natural growing process of the plant (fig. 23 and see fig. 22 on page 27).

The flowers need to be natural and vivid in posture, with charming branches, fresh petals, and unfolded leaves, capable of displaying the rhythmic beauty of a growing plant.

2. Emphasizing the Beauty of Lines

Painting started with line drawing both in the East and West. Western painting has developed along the thread of plane (color lump) composition while Chinese painting along the thread of line composition. Like Chinese painting, Chinese flower arrangement has also grown along the thread of line composition. Lines are the backbones of Chinese flower arrangement, which is thus known as "line flower arrangement" (fig. 23).

Lines are powerful in expression. Different lines will produce different visual effects on the viewers, stimulating them into different mental associations.

Straight lines can show uptrend, stubbornness, infuriation, vitality, force, righteousness, steadiness, and order.

Curved lines can display naturalness, elegance, gentleness, mellowness, cleverness, and grace.

Oblique lines can imply dynamism, breakthroughs, dashing, and adventure.

Fold lines can give a sense of staunchness, bravery, twists, ups and downs, and stubbornness.

Horizontal lines can show tranquility, stability, fluidity, and weightiness.

The rich connotations of lines offer a wide variety of topics for creative

Fig. 24 *Intoxicated in Autumn Wind*
Arrangement: Oriental bittersweet, sacred bamboo, chrysanthemum
Vessel: Pottery vase
Artist: Cai Zhongjuan

This work creates an enchanting scene of the golden October with yellow chrysanthemums amidst red leaves wavering in the intoxicating autumn wind. The branches of the oriental bittersweet are facile and graceful, accompanied by the dancing branches of the sacred bamboo. The red fruits and leaves set off by the golden yellow chrysanthemums offer the viewer an autumn scene of intoxicating charm. Of the four chrysanthemums, three are arranged in the front and one peeps out from the back, producing a hierarchical effect. The branches of the oriental bittersweet are gracefully curly, as if swaying in the wind. A branch links the vase from top to bottom, balancing the whole work.

Fig. 25 *Autumn Locked in a Deep Courtyard*
Arrangement: Red maple, common goldenrod herb, Chinese pink, asparagus myriocladus, bark
Vessel: Wooden frame
Artist: Cai Zhongjuan

This work is arranged in a picture frame, borrowing the "moon gate" and "window view" techniques in Chinese gardening. The picture frame resembles the window in a garden and the flowers resemble a corner of the garden view outside the window. The viewer can then appreciate the beautiful autumn scenes contained in a deep courtyard through the moon gate there. Though made up of simple materials, this work shows the big in the small, natural and vivid, poetic and picturesque.

flower arrangement. That is why in Chinese flower arrangement people are good at using tree branches and linear foliage of varied patterns for composition and design. Using the branches and foliage as the basic framework, they have created diversified works of flower arrangement with abundant themes (fig. 26).

3. Focusing on Artistic Conceptions

Chinese flower arrangement has grown from the flower arrangement practices of ancient men of letters, who were well-known poets, writers, calligraphic masters, and flower arrangement experts all rolled into one. Their profound learning and superior literary talent not only instilled the essence of aesthetics into flower arrangement, but also added to it rich connotations, thus greatly enhancing the cultural added values and artistic appeal of flower arrangement. Gradually, pursuing the implicit and abstruse essence of the work has become an important aspect of Chinese flower arrangement (fig. 25 and see fig. 21 on page 26).

The flower arrangements of scholars had always been closely related to poetry and painting. The scholars introduced poetic and pictorial splendor into flower arrangement and named their works in a way that could express their emotions and aspirations, so as to reach the highest aesthetic realm.

Apart from the above three basic characteristics, Chinese flower arrangement has many other characteristics, such as using the floral vessel to improve composition, expressing the best effect with a small number of materials, and giving priority to woody flowers.

A perfect work of flower arrangement should excel both in form and spirit. The form consists of the composition and color and the spirit is mirrored through the arranger's thoughts and feelings. An excellent work should have an enjoyable outlook, but more importantly, it should also be able to provide food for thought and inspire viewers to strive forward. Only in this way can it leave viewers with an indelible impression.

Fig. 26 *Listening to the Moon alongside a Brook*
Arrangement: Winged burning bush, Chinese juniper, crape myrtle, gmelin's sea lavender herb, chamomile, wood section, orpine
Vessel: Imitation porcelain plastic pot
Artist: Chen Juan

The leafless branches, graceful in shape, can constitute a beautiful landscape supported by well-chosen wood sections and autumn fruits and flowers. This work, slanting in posture, makes full use of the winged burning bush branches to express the charm of rustic life. The upper half displays the graceful beauty of the winding branches, the lower half uses the Chinese juniper as the bedding and the wood sections as the balance to enhance the density in the focal area and the strength of the base, and the middle part consists of some crape myrtles, gmelin's sea lavender herbs, and chamomile that add to the rustic interest of the work.

CHAPTER THREE
Basic Principles

In arranging flowers, Chinese artists must observe the law of aesthetics for artistic creations, take in the essence of literature to give the work a touch of inner beauty, and handle the plants appropriately based on a sound knowledge of their physiological and biological characteristics. In this sense, flower arrangement is a skill-based artistic creation.

For learners, they should be well-informed in picture composition, colors, flowers, and plants in general, be literature savvy, and even have a smattering of material science, optics, and mechanics, which, only when used comprehensively, can help produce better works.

On facing page
Fig. 27 *Clear Autumn*
Arrangement: Box, chamomile, Chinese St. John's wort fruit, dwarf lilyturf, asparagus myriocladus
Vessel: Porcelain vase
Artist: Cai Zhongjuan

After the scorching summer is over, people are expecting the refreshing autumn, which, to the Chinese, is a fine season with beautiful flowers and good harvests, symbolizing the perfect conjugal bliss of reunion and luck. The red fruits and white chamomile herald the coming of autumn while the swaying box branches and the leaves of the dwarf lilyturf create an intoxicating autumn scene. The green leaves and the red fruits are contrasted in color, which is offset by the white chamomile. The white color, which matches well with other colors, makes the whole work brighter.

Fig. 28 *Autumn Water and Clouds*
Arrangement: Lotus seed pod, lotus leaf, orpine, small wild flower, Amur silver grass
Vessel: Wooden frame
Artist: Cai Zhongjuan

The Amur silver grass on the left are void and light, looking like floating clouds. The lotus leaves and seed pods on the right are solid and heavy, staying firmly on the water surface. They constitute a vivid contrast. The dark red orpines on the lower left corner are supplemented by a group of yellow wild flowers at the bottom, displaying the scene of autumn harmoniously.

Fig. 29 *A Warm Spring Delights All Flowers*
Arrangement: Peony, oriental bush cherry, wax-leaf privet, gmelin's sea lavender herb, asparagus myriocladus, bark
Vessel: Pottery pot
Artist: Cai Zhongjuan

The flowers used in this work are wax-leaf privet with slender twigs and tender leaves, full-blown pink flowers of oriental bush cherry, beautiful peonies, and gmelin's sea lavender herbs with purple budding flowers. All these plants and flowers are infused with the salient features of spring. This work presents a beautiful view of spring with blooming flowers and elegant and graceful plants.

Fig. 30 *Dancing in Autumn Wind*
Arrangement: Amur silver grass, chrysanthemum, common goldenrod herb, asparagus myriocladus
Vessel: Wooden frame
Artist: Cai Zhongjuan

This work portrays autumn and the major materials chosen, such as Amur silver grass and chrysanthemums, are all typical of this season. The Amur silver grass, light and graceful, resemble the floating clouds in the sky. They echo the chrysanthemums on the earth from a far distance and greet each other in the beautiful autumn.

1. Principles of Composition

Flower arrangement is artistic creation. In order to display the theme and modeling effect of the work, the flower arranger must first make the composition, which is both an intellectual process that finds order among the disorderly things in nature and an organizing process that organizes the messy elements of composition into a unified whole. Like painters who organize on the canvas the dot, line, plane, colors, light, and shade following the spatial locations and musicians who arrange their instruments, musical rhythm, and melody following the chronological order, floriculturists organize flowers and floral vessels of different species, shapes, colors, and textures following the spatial locations. This is known as composition, or the art of composition.

Like artists of any other form of art, the flower arranger must observe the following principles of composition to achieve beauty in form.

Unity

The extremely abundant resources of plants in nature, such as the flowers, branches, stems, leaves, fruits, and sprouts, are the basis for achieving change in flower arrangement. Without changes, there will be no art to speak of. However, change must occur on a unified basis, or they will be loose and disorderly. On the contrary, unity without change is monotonous and rigid. Therefore, to maintain a fine balance between change and order, the flower arranger needs to achieve overall unity in his work. Specifically, unity in flower arrangement includes unity in theme, in style, and in material, floral vessels, and setting.

Unity in theme. The theme a work intends to express is the core of unity, based on which the floral vessels, flowers, colors, and flower patterns are chosen (figs. 29–30).

For example, if the theme is about spring sceneries, then spring flowers such as peach flowers, Chinese flowering crabapples, irises, and tulips could be chosen and the colors of the flowers can be pink, pastel yellow, and pinkish

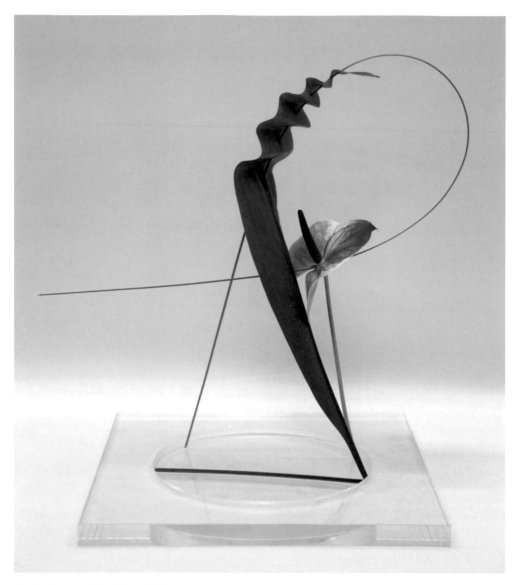

Fig. 31 *Innermost Thoughts and Feelings*
Arrangement: Anthurium, common aspidistra, steel grass
Vessel: Acrylic pot
Artist: Xie Ming

No fixing tools are used in this work. Instead, the artist has processed the flower, the leaf, and the grass to make them support each other in the shallow acrylic pot.

Following is how this work is created. Fold the upper end of a long and narrow common aspidistra leaf into the shape of a ladder. Choose a long blade of steel grass and pass it through the folded area of the common aspidistra leaf. Make a circle at the upper end of the steel grass and pass it through the middle of the common aspidistra leaf. The bottoms of the common aspidistra leaf and steel grass are leaned against the wall of the pot and are secured at the pot bottom. Place a bract of the anthurium on the steel grass and lean it against the common aspidistra leaf at the same time. Make it stand in the pot to balance the steel grass and the common aspidistra leaf.

This work, concisely designed, showcases the modern flower arrangement style typical of the East. It uses few plants but is unique in shape, incorporating many new elements in the use of the floral vessel and flowers and in composition.

purple, etc. If the theme is about autumn sceneries, then autumn flowers such as chrysanthemums, reed catkins, red maple, and pyracantha are good choices and the colors can be beige, golden yellow, brown, and red. This way, even though there are many flowers in a work, they are united as a whole.

Unity in style. Before he starts his flower arrangement, the flower arranger must first be crystal clear about which style his work will follow. For example, he must choose between the Eastern and Western styles, or the classical or modern styles. If he can choose different floral vessels and flowers based on a specific style, the work will look unified and harmonious (fig. 31 and see fig. 2 on pages 2 and 3).

Unity in material, floral vessels, and setting. The flowers must match the style, color, size, and function of the floral vessel as well as the setting to maximize the artistic effect. If the work is to be placed in a Chinese-style room with redwood furniture, the flower arranger can use as floral vessels traditional Chinese vases, pots, baskets, and bowls and urns, and can adopt the method of asymmetrical balance with woody flowers to make his work natural-looking. If the work is to be set in a modern setting, then fashionable floral vessels and bright-colored flowers can be used, supplemented with modern methods of Chinese flower arrangement (fig. 32).

Balance

Some works of flower arrangement aim at displaying the static beauty of dignity, elegance, and grace, and some, the dynamic beauty of dancing fluidity. For either purpose, the work should be visually balanced, since balance makes people feel safe and relaxed.

Chinese flower arrangement is based on careful observations of nature. The flower arranger often adopts the method of asymmetric balance to make his work natural and smooth. Very few things in nature, such as mountains, rivers, plants, clouds, and villages, are regular in form, but they constitute a beautiful and harmonious entity. Therefore, works of an asymmetrical composition can show more changes and demonstrate nature more efficiently (see fig. 33 on page 38).

Fig. 32 *Longing for a Brighter Future*
Arrangement: Anthurium, lily, dendrobium, philodendron, common goldenrod herb, leather leaf, and asparagus myriocladus
Vessel: Glass vase
Artist: Cai Zhongjuan

This is a modern work of flower arrangement using modern glassware. A receptacle with floral foam for arranging bouquet flowers is used at the mouth of the vase. The whole work is mainly line-shaped, but absorbs some modern floricultural techniques such as grouping and overlapping. This work is bright-colored and heartwarming, encouring the viewer to pursue a brighter future.

Contrast

Contrast as a method of flower arrangement is found almost at every stage, such as contrast in density, diffusion, size, curvature, length, solidness, pitching angles, and vitality. However, the flower arranger must also pay attention to overall harmony in making contrasts.

Contrast as a way to break away from uniformity and monotony in artistic creation refers to the use of changes and contrastive methods to give prominence to the image of a work, create visual impact, and increase its artistic appeal. For example, if a group of line flowers or mass flowers are placed on the upper right corner of a work, then on the upper left corner should be placed a group of lighter filler flowers to form contrast. Then on the lower right corner of the work can be placed a group of lighter flowers and on the lower left corner a group of heavier flowers. In this way, the two groups of flowers on the top and at the bottom contrast each other diagonally and coordinate with each other as well, creating a harmonious effect. Contrarily, if heavier flowers and lighter flowers are placed on the lower right corner and lower left corner respectively, the whole work will become weighty on the right and light on the left, lacking a sense of balance (fig. 34 and see fig. 28 on page 33).

Fig. 34 *Tranquility at the Pondside*
Arrangement: Calamus, blazing star, lily, pond lily, dendrobium, balloon flower, eustoma, leather leaf, paperplant, asparagus myriocladus
Vessel: Imitation porcelain plastic pot
Artist: Cai Zhongjuan

This work consists of four groups of flowers from left to right in two flower pots. The technique of contrast is adopted in many aspects. For example, in the first flower pot, the void calamus leaves contrast with the solid lilies, which contrast with the void balloon flowers and the leather leaves. There is also contrast between the third and fourth groups of flowers in the second flower pot, such as that between the solid blazing star and the void eustoma flowers and leather leaves and between the buds and flowers of the eustoma, which are void and solid, respectively.

The first group of flowers faces the fourth group of flowers across a distance and they also form a contrast between the void calamus leaves and the solid blazing star and between the solid lilies and the void eustoma flowers. Similarly, there is also contrast between the second and third groups of flowers, such as that between the void dendrobium and the solid pond lilies.

Contrast also exists in the colors of this work: the white lilies on the upper left corner echo the white eustoma flowers on the lower right corner and the indigo blazing star on the upper right corner coordinates with the blue balloon flowers on the lower left corner.

On facing page
Fig. 33 *A Tranquil Mind*
Arrangement: Calamus, golden-leaf elm, calla, bell flower
Vessel: Porcelain pot
Artist: Cai Zhongjuan

In this work, the calamus leaves serve as the axis line. On its right is a longer branch of the golden-leaf elm and a bigger number of the bell flowers. They balance the two heavy callas on the upper left corner. The small leaves of the golden-leaf elm peep out from behind the calamus leaves, enriching the hierarchical effect of the work. In Chinese flower arrangement, there may not be many flowers and leaves, but each of them should be vigorous and agile, natural and charming.

Rhythm

Music has rhythms and poetry has meters, both of which are produced with the repeated rhythmic changes of sound. Though rhythms and meters come from music and poetry, they are now used in various other forms of art and are among the elements that produce the beauty of harmony. Likewise, flower arrangement displays rhythms through changes in height, length, density, depth, etc. Such a floral work is stratified and rich in variation (fig. 35).

Fig. 35   *An Impression of Zhangjiajie*
Arrangement: Bark, sawara cypress, common goldenrod herb, gmelin's sea lavender herb, Chinese pink, and asparagus myriocladus
Vessel: Imitation porcelain plastic pots
Artist: Cai Zhongjuan

Using barks and other materials, this work is an imitation of the towering mountain ranges in China's Zhangjiajie Forest Park in Hunan Province. The peaks and trees are appropriately spaced and harmonious in heights, exhibiting rhythmic changes.

Proportion

In flower arrangement, being proportional is the main characteristic of beauty in form. It is often realized by adopting the golden section proportion, which consists of the following five aspects. Please be noted that in the illustrations presented below, "b" is short for breadth while "h" for height.

Proportion in overall design. The proportion between the height and breadth of an upright, slanting, or pendent floral work is often 8:5 while that between the breadth and height of a horizontal or semi-pendent work is also 8:5. This proportion (or approximately 5:3 or 3:2) is often regarded as the golden section proportion, which can be found everywhere in our daily lives, such as the proportion of a TV set, office desk, notebook, soapbox, etc., because it is visually the most comfortable and with the widest application (figs. 36–37).

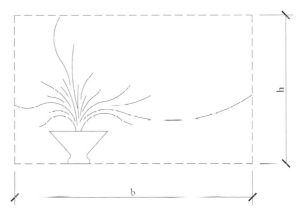

Fig. 37   The horizontal composition between the breadth and height of the work is 1.618:1, which is equivalent to 5:8.

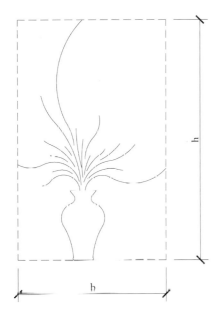

Fig. 36   The vertical composition between the breadth and height of the work is 1:1.618, which is equivalent to 8:5.

Proportion between the flowers and the floral vessel. A good knowledge of the proportion between the flowers and the floral vessel means that one has mastered a greater part of the overall proportion of a work. If the flowers are arranged in a flower pot, the height of the longest flower branch should be 1.5 or 2 times the sum of the breadth and height of the flower pot (see fig. 38 on page 42). If the flowers are arranged in a vase, the height of the longest flower branch should be 1.5 or 2 times the sum of the height and breadth of the vase. This proportion is also applicable to flower arrangement in baskets, bamboo tubes, or other floral vessels (see fig. 39 on page 42).

Though commonly used, this proportion is certainly not absolute and can be adjusted based on the depth of the flower pot, the size of the vase, or the density of the flowers. Flower arrangement is not as precise as machine

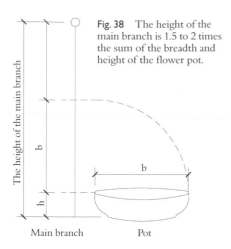

Fig. 38 The height of the main branch is 1.5 to 2 times the sum of the breadth and height of the flower pot.

The height of the main branch

b

h

Main branch   Pot

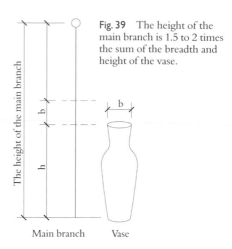

Fig. 39 The height of the main branch is 1.5 to 2 times the sum of the breadth and height of the vase.

The height of the main branch

b

b

h

Main branch   Vase

building, whose proportions can never be altered. It is an artistic creation aiming at achieving visual comfort.

Proportion between the three main branches. The Chinese flower arranger mainly adopts the asymmetrical composition. At the initial stage, he often uses three main branches to set up the frame of his work. The first main branch is normally the longest one, which determines the basic posture of the work, either upright, slanting, pendent, or horizontal. The second main branch is about two thirds of the first main branch in length and the third main branch is about two thirds of the second main branch in length. The three main branches can form scalene triangles with countless changes and between the three will generate many golden ratio relations (figs. 40–41).

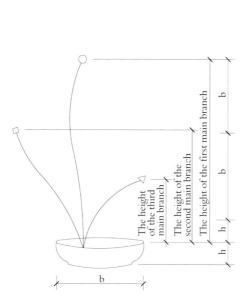

Fig. 40 The proportion between the three main branches of the pot flower, which serves as a reference when other vessels are used for flower arrangement.

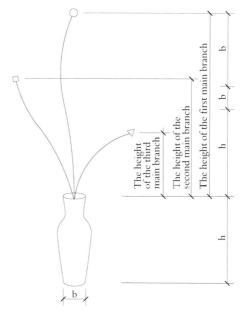

Fig. 41 The proportion between the three main branches of the vase flower, which serves as a reference when other vessels are used for flower arrangement.

Proportion of the focus. The focus of a floral work is its visual center, also known as the Center of Interest, which is often located near the point of the golden section proportion and is one third of the main branch in height. Since the focus is the visual center, it makes the whole work balanced (figs. 42–43).

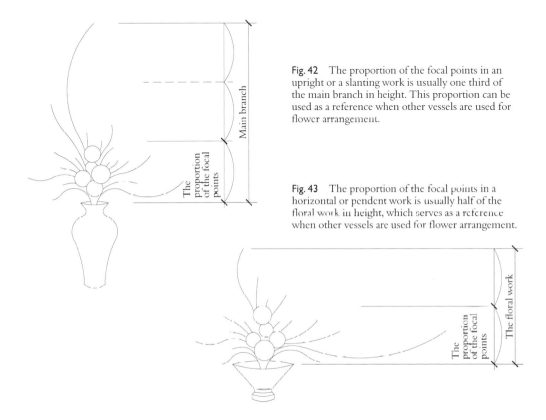

Fig. 42 The proportion of the focal points in an upright or a slanting work is usually one third of the main branch in height. This proportion can be used as a reference when other vessels are used for flower arrangement.

Fig. 43 The proportion of the focal points in a horizontal or pendent work is usually half of the floral work in height, which serves as a reference when other vessels are used for flower arrangement.

Proportion between the work and its setting. The flower arranger should not only coordinate between the aforementioned proportions, but should also handle well the proportion between the work and the setting it is in. A large work in a narrow space will give the viewers a sense of cramming and oppression and a small work in a large space will make them feel imbalanced. Therefore, arranging flowers is like making a dress, which must be tailored-made. Or in other words, the proportion of a work is determined by where it is placed.

Sometimes, to suit the work with the setting, the flower arranger is justified to make some technical adjustments. For example, in the case where the space is big while the work is small, he can use a screen, wall frame, picture frame, or window frame to expand the overall visual effect.

Fig. 44 *Spring Grass in a Pond*
Arrangement: Calamus, iris, Chinese pink, paperplant (with leaves cut into the shape of lily pad)
Vessel: Imitation porcelain plastic pot
Artist: Cai Zhongjuan

At the time when spring and summer meet, the calamus are extending their leaves and the lily pads are taking into shape. This work portrays a scene of limpid pond water enveloped in emerald green, making the viewers feel nice and cool. The three bunches of calamus leaves are in picturesque disorder, with the tallest on the left, the lowest in the middle, and the medium-sized on the right. The same order is adopted in each of the three bunches as well. The four irises are also arranged in disorder, and so are the Chinese pinks and small leaves of paperplant, showing asymmetric balance in all respects.

2. Rules of Shape-Designing

Normally, six rules of shape-designing are found in Chinese flower arrangement.

Variation in Height

This is a rule students of Chinese flower arrangement must bear in mind, because as mentioned previously, most sceneries in nature, such as mountains, rivers, and plants, are basically irregular in form, but they coexist harmoniously. This is echoed by Yuan Hongdao in *History of Vases*. According to him, the various heights of the plants in a vase produce naturalness and changes. In other words, the flowers should be arranged in picturesque order, with various heights and positions, instead of horizontally or vertically without any discrimination. In case the flowers or the ends of the branches form a regular straight, horizontal, or oblique line, the overall compatibility of the work would be destroyed and the work would require further adjustment (fig. 44).

Combining the Solid and the Void

In flower arrangement, the arranger should handle the solid and the void appropriately, because this can make his work natural and vivid, balanced and harmonious.

The major ways to combine the solid and the void are as follows:

Flowers being the solid and leaves the void. Flowers are often set off by the green leaves. In flower arrangement, the flower arranger needs to fill in the void with either flowers or leaves as he sees fit. Properly used, leaves can set off the flowers more charmingly. The many kinds of leaves in nature expand the scope of flower arrangement (fig. 45).

Fig. 45 *In Admiration*
Arrangement: Calla, common aspidistra, eustoma, leather leaf
Vessel: Porcelain vase
Artist: Cai Zhongjuan

The callas are graceful and elegant, while the eustoma beneath seem to be looking up in admiration. Beautiful as the flowers are, they need green leaves to prop them up, which is done perfectly by the common aspidistra leaves and leather leaves. Some works of flower arrangement are very concise in form, but conciseness does not mean mere simplicity. A work is extraordinary if it is done appropriately.

Full-blown flowers being the solid and buds the void. The same kind of flowers may differ in size due to time of blossoming. The full-blown ones, which are large and bright-colored, are often placed in the focal area, while the buds, which are small and light-colored, are used as supplements (see *Divine Beauty* on page 167).

Flowers in the front being the solid and those in the back the void. In nature, flowers mostly blossom towards the sun, with some against or alongside it. In flower arrangement, while the flowers are mostly placed in the front, some should appear in the back or sideways to fill in the void. This way, the whole work looks more natural and lively (fig. 46).

Blocky flowers being the solid and line-shaped ones the void. In Chinese flower arrangement, line flowers are often used as the frame, while blocky flowers are placed in the focal area. In a work of asymmetric balance, long branches are often used on one side and short branches on the other, forming a contrast between the solid and the void and achieving balance and harmony (fig. 47).

Heavy flowers being the solid and light ones the void. Apart from the size, length, and shape, the weight of the flowers also contributes to a contrast between the solid and the void. Generally, the top and the exterior are the void and the bottom and interior are the solid. If one side is treated as the void, the other side is the solid (see fig. 48 on page 48).

Appropriateness in Distance

Chinese flower arrangement resembles Chinese painting which emphasizes changes in distance. The whole work must be appropriate in space allocation, with some plants closely together and others at a proper distance. Space allocation based on equal distance should be avoided.

Normally, flowers in the focal area of a work should be closer to each other than those in the frame area. In a work of asymmetric balance, when flowers on one side

Fig. 46 *Demeanor of Noble Family*
Arrangement: Black coral, barbados lily, ceriman, vine
Vessel: Pottery vase
Artist: Cai Zhongjuan

The barbados lilies either face the front, the back or right and left. Some of them are in full blossom and some in buds, showing the natural growing process of the flowers.

Fig. 47 *Intoxicated in the Light of Spring*
Arrangement: Rock cotoneaster, peony, paperplant
Vessel: Porcelain vase
Artist: Cai Zhongjuan

With curly and vigorous branches and thin and tiny leaves, the rock cotoneaster looks graceful and is an ideal material for frame construction. Visually empty, it matches excellently with the paperplant leaves and peonies that look heavy and solid.

are closer, those on the other side should be more distant. In a work to be viewed from one side, flowers in the front should be closer than those in the back. Even for flowers in the same position, whether they are in the frame, supplementary, or focal areas, they should be varied in distance and same-distance arrangement should be avoided. This is comparable to trees in a park.

For natural charm, most trees, except for those at the roadsides, are planted in varied distances; some are closely together, some in isolation, and still some far apart from each other(see *Slanting Branches of Purple Magnolia* on page 156).

The Bottom Echoing the Top

Flowers have their own directions of blooming and branches their own directions of bending. Therefore, in flower arrangement, the flower arranger should make full use of these directions to achieve the best result. Normally, the flower in the focal area is the center and all the other flowers will circle around it, like a myriad of stars surrounding the moon. This arrangement not only exhibits the life of the flowers vividly, but also directs the attention of the viewer to the focal area and enhances the steadiness of the whole work (see fig. 122 on page 114).

Light at the Top and Weighty at the Bottom

To make the work steady and secure, the flower arranger usually makes it light on the top and weighty at the bottom. For example, the buds, small flowers, spike flowers, and light-colored flowers are often placed at the top, while the full-blown flowers, big flowers, blocky flowers, and dark-colored flowers appear at the bottom. Similarly, in an pendent or horizontal work, the flowers in the focal area are the biggest and the farther a flower is from the focal area, the smaller it will be. In other words, if the flowers are arranged from the frame to the focal area, then the flowers will change from small into big, and vice versa (see *Graceful and Unrestrained* on page 160).

Though this rule is commonly used, it is by no means absolute. So long as the whole work is balanced and harmonious, one can also arrange the flowers the other way around.

Fanning Out at the Top and Concentrated at the Bottom

Externally, a work needs to be fluent and colorful, but the bottom of the flowers needs to be closely concentrated, as if the flowers grew from the same root. This rule is formulated to simulate nature and has been emphasized since ancient time.

Whatever floral vessels or fixers that might be used in flower arrangement, the top of the work must fan out while the bottom must be concentrated at one point. Only when this is skillfully applied can the work look natural and complete (see fig. 102 on page 96).

On facing page
Fig. 48 *In Mist*
Arrangement: Smoke tree, photinia fraseri, freesia, blue throatwort, tree section
Vessel: Imitation porcelain plastic pot
Artist: Cai Zhongjuan

The two clusters of smoke tree flowers are illusory, light and graceful, looking like smoke and mist. They are arranged on the top and at the bottom, slanting towards the left and right, respectively, and with space in the middle. On the left side of the smoke tree flowers is a cluster of photinia fraseri and freesia flowers, behind which is a thicket of dark purple blue throatwort flower, which intensifies the overall setting. As the freesia and smoke tree flowers are similar in color, they integrate with each other naturally while showing changes. The photinia fraseri, with big leaves and gorgeous flowers, are overall coordinated with the smoke tree flowers in color. They also form a vivid contrast with the smoke tree flowers in weight. The tree sections at the base add to the rustic flavor of the work.

Fig. 49 *Radiant Autumn Chrysanthemums*
Arrangement: Red maple, chrysanthemum, chamomile, paperplant
Vessel: Bamboo basket
Artist: Cai Zhongjuan

This work, arranged in a brown flower basket, is harmonious in color, with the red maple as its frame and the dark red chamomile as the supplement. The several yellow chrysanthemums in the focal area are vivid and pleasant-looking. The paperplants are used as the background, rendering the focal area more solid. With well-chosen colors and materials, this work depicts most vividly the charm of autumn.

3. Color Allocation

Chinese flower arrangement follows the way of nature, the color of which is often determined by the original color of the flower selected, such as pink peach flowers, scarlet pomegranates, white pear blossoms, red peonies, etc.

Since color plays a pivotal role in the beauty of a work, it must be designed in accordance with aesthetic laws, so that the work derives from nature and is yet on a higher plane than nature itself. Following are some rules of color allocation in Chinese flower arrangement.

Conformity to the Theme
If the theme is about spring sceneries, the main colors of the flowers should be light, such as pink, yellow, purple, and green. If it is about autumn sceneries, then the main colors should be yellow, orange, and brown (fig. 49).

If the theme is about untamed passion, the main colors should be red and orange. If it is about tranquility and plainness, then the main colors should be light blue, light purple, light green, and white.

Fig. 50 *Bluish-Green*
Arrangement: Snow willow, green cabomba, paphiopedilum, asparagus myriocladus
Vessel: Wooden frame
Artist: Cai Zhongjuan

This work consists of different materials of the green color. However, the color varies between greenish yellow, tender green, light green, and greenish black, rich but well-coordinated. Meanwhile, the artist has borrowed the technique of the enframed scenery commonly found in Chinese gardening. Looking exactly like a fan leaf painting, this work is best appreciated on a table or on the wall.

Overall Harmony

Flower arrangement requires many kinds of harmony in color allocation, such as harmony between different flowers, between flowers and the floral vessel, between the work and the setting it is in, etc.

Color collocation using single colors (referring to the gradation changes of the same color, e.g. light green, green, deep green, and greenish black), similar colors (e.g. lemon yellow, medium yellow, and light yellow), colors of the same category (referring to the collocation between two adjacent colors, e.g. red and orange, red and purple, yellow and orange, blue and green, blue and purple, etc.) produces secondary color, which can lead to overall harmony more conveniently (figs. 50–51).

Fig. 51 *Elegance*
Arrangement: Moth orchids, chamomile, baby's breath, hydrangea, bamboo slip (note: all are imitation flowers)
Vessel: Pottery vase
Artist: Cai Zhongjuan

This work uses same-category colors. The various shades of blue are the dominant color, which is set off by the white focal flowers. The whole work looks refreshing and pure, elegant and tranquil.

The blue vase in this work is a rectangular white vase sprayed with the blue color. Of course, you can also use a similar blue vase. On the surface of the vase are blue chamomile and white baby's breath sticked with hot melt adhesive. Inside the vase is some dry floral foam and at the mouth of the vase are two fan-shaped frames made of deep-blue and light-blue bamboo slips. The moth orchids are located in the focal area, supplemented by hydrangea and blue chamomiles in the front, at the back, and between the two frames to enrich the hierarchy. The whole work looks noble and elegant.

Fig. 52 *Emerald Green by a Creek*
Arrangement: Calamus, willow herb, Chinese rose, balloon flower, eustoma, common goldenrod herb, Chinese pink, leather leaf
Vessel: Imitation porcelain plastic pot
Artist: Cai Zhongjuan

The depth of the color can have different visual effects. Generally, the light color produces a lighter effect than the dark color. Therefore, balance in color is important in flower arrangement and light colors on one side and dark colors on the other side should best be avoided. In this work, the flowers on the left side are light-colored at the top and dark-colored at the bottom while those on the right are exactly the opposite, thus achieving visual balance on the whole.

Fig. 53 *Status and Wealth*
Arrangement: Peony, Chinese herbaceous peony, camellia
Vessel: Bamboo basket
Artist: Cai Zhongjuan

Peonies are bright-colored, graceful, regal, and fragrant. They have always been a symbol of auspiciousness, happiness, and prosperity. There are six branches of peonies and Chinese herbaceous peonies in the basket, the white Chinese herbaceous peonies above, the purple one below, and the pink peonies in the middle. The whole work looks steady and dignified.

If contrastive colors (e.g. red and green, yellow and purple, and blue and orange) or multiple colors are used, there must be a main color and all the other colors should set off the main color or add the finishing touch to it. Efforts should be made to coordinate different colors and allocate them most appropriately (see fig. 27 on page 32).

The transition between different colors should be natural. There should be some intersections at where different colors meet, so as not to give the viewers a feeling of obvious incision.

Emphasis on Balance
The gradation of color will produce a feeling of visual weightiness. In flower arrangement, the light color is often arranged on the top and the dark color at the bottom to enhance the steadiness of the work. If it is the opposite case, there should be more light-color flowers or the light color should depend on the support of dark-colored foliage, floral vessels, or wood sections to gain balance (fig. 53).

Fig. 54 *Singing in a Low Voice*
Arrangment: Pyracantha, cymbidium, chrysanthemum, paperplant, dwarf lilyturf, leather leaf
Vessel: Bamboo tube and bamboo basket
Artist: Cai Zhongjuan

This work uses both a bamboo tube and a bamboo basket. The light-green cymbidiums above the top opening of the bamboo tube echo diagonically the light-green chrysanthemums in the bamboo basket. Besides, the dark-red color in the centers of the cymbidiums also matches perfectly the dark-red chrysanthemums in the lower opening of the bamboo tube. Similarly, the dark-green pyracantha branches on the left side of the top opening of the bamboo tube and the dark-green dwarf lilyturf leaves on the right side of the bamboo basket are also well-matched. The work is harmonious and coordinated either in color or in composition. Using simple and unadorned floral vessels and flowers, this work implies that one should keep a low profile and has moral integrity.

The colors on the right and left sides of the work should also be balanced. If one side is just a light color and another side just a dark color, then the work is not balanced. Overall balance in color can be achieved only when the dark color on one side echoes the light color on the other side or when they coordinate with each other obliquely, for example, the dark color is on the upper left and the light color on the lower right, or the dark color is on the upper right and the light color on the lower left (fig. 54 and see fig. 52 on page 52).

4. Conception Determination and Naming

Flower arrangement is an artistic work that can take on a life of its own. Determining the conception of a work and naming it are of paramount importance. In the following, I will discuss the characteristics and methods of conception determination and naming.

Two Major Characteristics

Artistic flower arrangement focuses on beauty in form and in artistic conception. The former is displayed by the flowers, floral vessels, molding, and colors used. The latter depends on the flowers, floral vessels, molding, colors, and settings to express emotions and life goals, aiming at inspiring the viewers into pursuing a better future and bringing the work to a new height of artistic satisfaction.

A Stress on artistic conceptions. Chinese art has always emphasized the creation and appreciation of artistic conceptions, which culminates in ancient Chinese poetry and painting that expressed the author's intention and feelings with concise language or brush strokes. The techniques often used are simple language and broad thinking that enabled the viewers to see beyond the painting and poetry. The so-called poetic and pictorial splendor does not merely mean writing a poem on a piece of painting, but the poetization of the painting and the pictorializing of the poem. In other words, the author tries to present broad topics and far-reaching artistic conceptions through the use of the most concise language, aiming to trigger limitless imaginations within limited space.

It is justified to say that the creation and appreciation of artistic conceptions have been engraved into the aesthetic psychology of the Chinese people. They are closely related to the time-honored history and profound cultural deposits of China and the reserved national character of the Chinese and are the natural result of a long historical accumulation and deep cultural sedimentation.

An unlimited number of artistic conceptions. A work of flower arrangement can express a single artistic conception or multiple artistic conceptions from different angles. For example, a work with the chrysanthemum as the main flower can depict sceneries in autumn or symbolize one's later years of life and indomitable character.

The proper display of the artistic conception of a floral work lies not only with the flower arranger, but also with the viewer. Their understanding of the artistic conception is determined by their own education, artistic cultivation, knowledge and experience, and personal tastes.

Basic Methods of Artistic Conception Determination

The artistic conceptions of flower arrangement vary greatly, but the methods used to determine them are of the following two.

Fig. 55 *The Drunken Beauty*
Arrangement: Peony, magnolia, haw (note: all are imitation flowers)
Vessel: Irregularly-shaped pottery vessel
Artist: Cai Zhongjuan

This vessel is irregular in shape, consisting of three smaller vases. It constitutes an intoxicating view together with the graceful magnolias. The peonies in the focal area are big and brilliantly red. Since the peony is a symbol of the Tang Dynasty, this work reminds the viewer of the natural and graceful dancing postures of a drunken beauty in Peking opera.

Determining the artistic conception before getting started. This means that the flower arranger conceives the artistic conception of the work before he begins. He may need to determine the theme of his work first, and then draw a sketch map and specify the flowers, floral vessels, and colors to be used. Or he may need to choose the flowers, floral vessels, and colors based on the set theme, and then draw a sketch map on which he could start arranging the flowers (fig. 55).

With this advance careful deliberation, it is easy for such a work to become ideally mature.

Fig. 56 *A Colorful Phoenix Descending from Heaven*
Arrangement: Wisteria, lilac, calla, bell flower, leather leaf, asparagus myriocladus, iris leaf
Vessel: Imitation porcelain plastic pot
Artist: Cai Zhongjuan

This is a pot flower with a slanting posture. On the left side of the wisteria are arranged several branches of lilacs, the pattern and color of which are different from but unified with the wisteria flowers. Since the stems of the wisteria and lilacs are bare and void at the bottom, iris leaves and leather leaves are used to enrich the right side and the left and rear. The callas serve as the focal flowers, the bell flowers as the supplement, and the asparagus myriocladus as the ornament. The several branches of budding wisteria flowers look exactly like colorful phoenixes descending from heaven, bringing auspiciousness and happiness.

Determining the artistic conception based on the materials available. This means that the flower arranger does not have a specific theme in advance. He could conceive the artistic conception of his work while arranging the flowers or he could arrange the flowers first and then name the work. Since the flowers in nature (especially the tree branches) vary greatly, he could not possibly design everything beforehand, but can endow his work with a conception on the spot based on the materials available.

Fig. 57 *Elegance*
Arrangement: Iris leaf, lily, eustoma, dwarf lilyturf, calla leaf
Vessel: Imitation porcelain plastic bowl
Artist: Cai Zhongjuan

This work is refreshing in color, with the white lilies as the focal flowers, supplemented by the green iris and calla leaves and dotted by the purple-blue eustoma flowers. The upright posture is concise and elegant, offering the viewers a sense of leisurely tranquility.

Methods of Naming a Work

A work can be named in one word, a phrase, an idiom, a line of poetry, a tale, an allusion, or a literary term. Specifically, the following factors need to be considered in naming a work.

The allegorical meaning or the shape of the main flowers. Since flowers differ in shape and nature and in their ability to withstand natural disasters, people bestow them with different connotations, sometimes based on related historical events, thus giving them symbolic meanings or personifying them (see fig. 52 on page 57 and fig. 60 on page 62).

The composition of the work. Chinese flower arrangement is mainly line-shaped. The different kinds of lines will stimulate different mental associations and offer different visual effects (see fig. 104 on page 98).

The colors of the work. Colors have symbolic meanings and produce emotional effects. For example, red symbolizes brightness, warmth, vitality, excitement, enthusiasm, happiness, youth, and kindness, but on the other hand it relates to warning, aggression, and terror. Orange symbolizes brightness, magnificence, nobleness, maturity, health, excitement, warmth, splendor, and anxiety. Yellow symbolizes brightness, hope, splendor, light-heartedness, briskness, gentleness, decadency, and morbidity. Green symbolizes life, hope, spring, peace, luxuriance, grace, and sentimentality. Blue symbolizes tranquility, purity, freshness, deepness, aloofness and sadness. Purple symbolizes nobleness, elegance, superiority, and unsettledness. White symbolizes purity,

Fig. 58 *Peerless in Beauty and Elegance*
Arrangement: Anthurium, sophora japonica, camellia branch, common goldenrod herb, asparagus myriocladus
Vessel: Bamboo tube
Artist: Cai Zhongjuan

Like *Elegance* (fig. 65), this work is also named based on its color. However, it is brighter and, with vigorous branches, looks more enthusiastic and dashing.

Fig. 59 *Indistinct Moon, Indistinct Flowers*
Arrangement: Chinese tamarisk, chrysanthemum, paperplant
Vessel: Wooden frame
Artist: Cai Zhongjuan

Using a round picture frame, this work portrays a beautiful scene in the legendary moon palace featuring graceful flowers and clear wind under cloudy moonlight. The round hollow in the picture frame resembles a bright moon in the dark night sky that sets off the green chrysanthemums and Chinese tamarisk. The Chinese tamarisk is a small deciduous tree ideal for sand retaining. Its branches are long and thin and its leaves are as fine as silk. Together they create a visual effect of indistinctness.

brightness, briskness, freshness, coolness, and distress. Black symbolizes stateliness, glory, solemnity, mystery, gloom, and terror (see figs. 57–58 on pages 58 and 59).

The floral vessels. The floral vessels, stands, and small ornaments for flower arrangements are many, whose shapes, colors, and textures can inspire the flower arranger with the best name for his work (fig. 59 and see fig. 3 on page 6).

The integrated conditions of the work. Many works express the themes with integrated elements, such as the flowers, compositions, floral vessels, colors, and settings, which enhance the impact of the themes and help to achieve overall harmony and good artistic effects (figs. 69–70).

How to Improve on Attainment in Conception Determination and Naming

Although there are methods to improve on attainment in conception determination and naming, more important is that the flower arranger can constantly improve his cultural and artistic attainments, which cannot be achieved instantaneously, but requires years of learning and accumulation. Generally, one can start from the following aspects.

Improving on cultural accomplishment. As artistic flower arrangement produces works with cultural content, the flower arranger must improve on his cultural accomplishment, cultivate his aesthetic tastes, and broaden his scope of appreciation. Only in this way can he improve his ability of appreciation and artistic creation.

Increasing the knowledge of flowers. Chinese flower arrangement emphasizes the expression of the artistic conception, a concept established on the cultural deposits accumulated through thousands of years. For example, plum blossoms, orchids, bamboos, and chrysanthemums, which are known as the Four Gentlemen in Chinese culture, represent pride, calm, determination, and simplicity, and are extensively used in poetry, painting, and flower arrangement. Like the four flowers, other flowers, in fact, also have their human qualities. The profound Chinese floriculture is a precious cultural heritage and an inexhaustible treasure house for artistic creations in Chinese flower arrangement.

Apart from the spiritual properties bestowed by people, flowers also have their physiological and ecological properties, such as their enological phases, growing environments, abilities to fend off natural disasters, textures, etc.

The more knowledge one has about the natural and human qualities of flowers, the more easily he will make mental associations at the time of conception determination and naming, and the more relevance he will be able to apply to the theme.

Gathering related knowledge. The topics one can use for flower arrangement are many. He can expand his train of thought in conception determination and naming by borrowing from other forms of art, such as poetry and painting, music, movies, literature, opera, gardening, *penjing*, stone appreciation, and industrial arts.

Observing nature and society. Nature and society are the sources of creation in flower arrangement. A good flower arranger will be able to give prominence to what is positive and beautiful by integrating into his work the fine aspects of nature and society.

Undeniably, the flower arranger is both a creator of beauty and a disseminator of culture. Only when he keeps improving his own cultural and artistic qualities and gather related knowledge from all sides can he produce fine works with good artistic conceptions.

CHAPTER FOUR
Basic Postures

There are four basic postures in Chinese flower arrangement: upright, slanting, pendent, and horizontal. It is also possible to combine them for other new postures. The basic posture of a work is often determined by the angle and posture of the first main branch (the longest flower branch in the work).

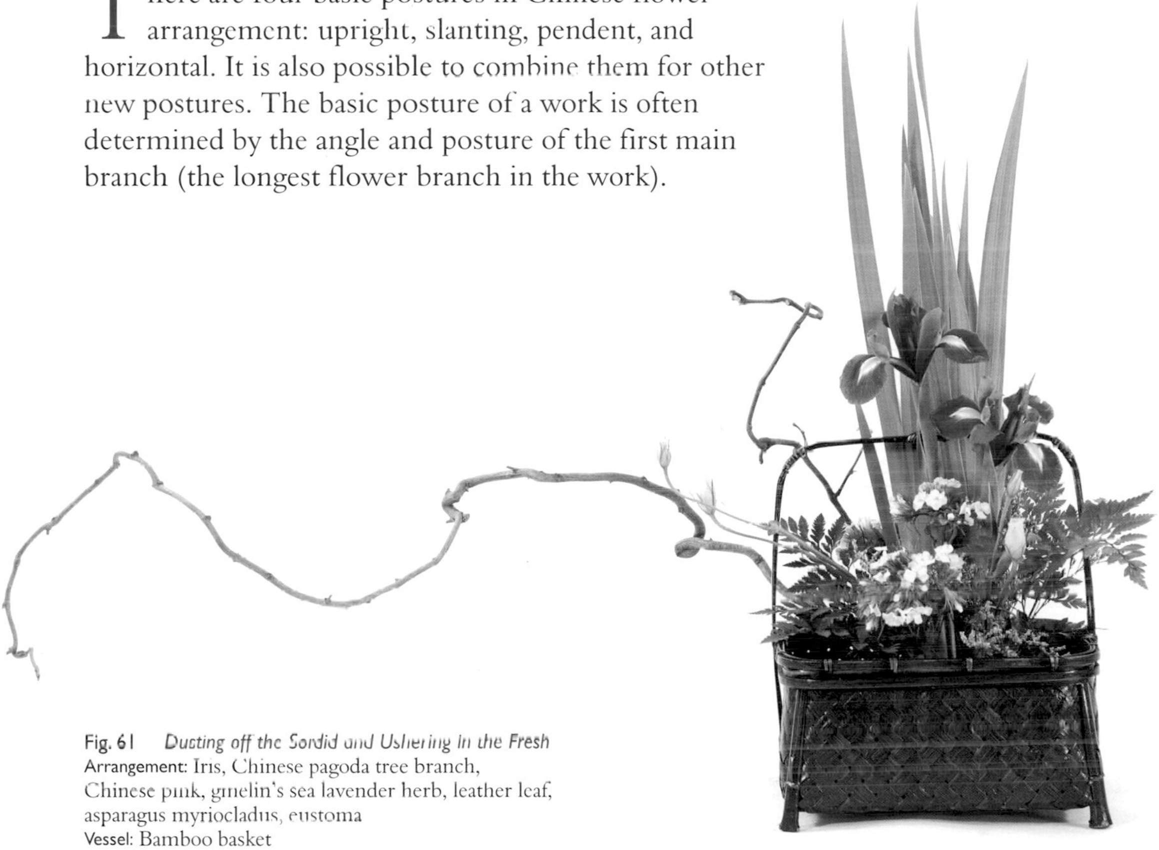

Fig. 61 *Dusting off the Sordid and Ushering in the Fresh*
Arrangement: Iris, Chinese pagoda tree branch, Chinese pink, gmelin's sea lavender herb, leather leaf, asparagus myriocladus, eustoma
Vessel: Bamboo basket
Artist: Cai Zhongjuan

This is a horizontal work. A graceful branch of the Chinese pagoda tree serves as the main stem that extends to the left horizontally. It is enriched at the bottom by another shorter branch. A cluster of iris leaves and leather leaves serve as the frame. The two irises that are varied in height are arranged in the focal area, with the Chinese pinks and gmelin's sea lavender herbs as the supplement and the asparagus myriocladus as the ornament. Several eustoma flowers add to the dynamic of the focal flowers.

The whole work is elegant in color and steadfast in structure. The branch of the Chinese pogada tree reaches out like the sleeve of a Buddist monk dusting off the sordid and usher in the fresh.

On facing page
Fig. 60 *Riches and Honors*
Arrangement: Magnolia, Chinese flowering crabapple, Chinese herbaceous peony, paperplant
Vessel: Porcelain vase
Artist: Cai Zhongjuan

In ancient times, for good luck, artists of flower arrangement often used homophony in naming their works. In this work, the magnolia is homophonic with "jade" in Chinese pronounciation and the Chinese flowering crabapple with "hall" and the Chinese herbaceous peonies symbolize wealth and power. Therefore, the name of this work connotes the meaning of having riches and honors.

1. Upright

The first main branch is basically upright, tilting within 15° to the vertical axis on the right or left (fig. 62).

Such a work looks tall and straight, dignified and magnanimous. It is full of vitality, embodying static beauty (fig. 63).

In making such a work, one can use linear materials that are tall and straight as the first main branch, such as the white willow, red twig dogwood, lucky bamboo, cordyline fruticosa, bamboo, sacred bamboo, reed, calamus, cattail, scirpus tabernaemontani, willow herb, tuberose, blazing star, strelitzia, Chinese rose, iris, calla, and chrysanthemum. He can also choose woody branches that are close to uprightness, such as the Chinese flowering crabapple and magnolia.

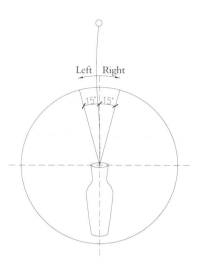

Fig. 62　The upright posture.

Fig. 63 *Rebirth*
Arrangement: Chinese tamarisk, smartweed, iris, common goldenrod herb, chamomile, leather leaf, decadent branch, tree section
Vessel: Imitation porcelain plastic pot
Artists: Xu Guodong, Jiang Zhiling, and Liu Xin

This work is of an upright posture. The first main branch is the upright Chinese tamarisk, which is taller than all the other materials used. The surface of the flower pot is covered with decadent branches, tree sections, and pebbles. At the bottom are some wild flowers and grasses, which rid the work of any trace of the human touch and create the most natural effect.

2. Pendent

The first main branch is basically pendent, tilting 15° below the horizontal axis on the right or left sides. The pendent side is often on the right or left side of the floral vessel (fig. 64).

A pendent work looks dynamic, brisk, and bold. The hanging vines and foliage resemble currents of water flowing down from the mountaintop, giving the viewers a strong sense of dynamic beauty (figs. 65–66).

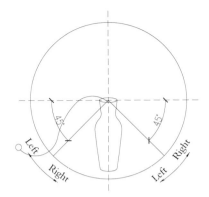

Fig. 64   The pendent posture.

Such a work requires a naturally curving branch with gentle leaves and long twigs as the first main branch, such as the wisteria, grape, Chinese gooseberry, ivy, periwinkle, snow willow, winter jasmine, orchid leaf, dwarf lilyturf, snowrose, barberry, star jasmine, contorted willow, jujube, or the processed white willow, calla, and anthurium.

Fig. 65   *Spring Wind along the Road*
Arrangement: Snowrose, Chinese rose, meadowsweet, leather leaf
Vessel: Bamboo basket
Artist: Cai Zhongjuan

Three branches of snowrose serve as the three main branches. The first main branch declines towards the right, the end of which is above the table. Another branch is added at the bottom of the first main branch as the enrichment. The second main branch is arranged on the upper left of the work to echo the first main branch from above. The third main branch extends to the left, balancing the first two main branches. Several branches of leather leaves are arranged at the bottom of the snowrose, which not only usher in the floral flowers but also serve as a transition between the frame and the focal point.

The bright yellow Chinese roses in this work resemble girls in their early teens, who seem to be appreciating the beauty of spring along the road, accompanied by the graceful branches of snowrose swaying in the wind. This work is a good combination of activity and inertia.

Fig. 66   *Charm of Spring*
Arrangement: Snowrose, Chinese herbaceous peony, Chinese astilbe, paperplant, asparagus myriocladus
Vessel: Porcelain vase
Artist: Cai Zhongjuan

The pruned snowrose branch, which serves as the first main branch, is declining towards the right, with its far end bending upwards. On the upper right side is arranged another snowrose branch, which serves as the second main branch. Tilting towards the left at the upper part, it pulls the center of gravity of this work back to the center. The paperplants on the left serve as the third main branch, balancing the first and second main branches. The Chinese herbaceous peonies are the focal flowers, supplemented by the Chinese astilbes. The asparagus myriocladus is for embellishment.

The Chinese herbaceous peonies are big and magnificent, displaying the static beauty to the fullest. Together with the dancing snowrose branches, they strike a fine balance between activity and inertia and exhibit the charm of spring most perfectly.

Fig. 67 *Dancing Gracefully in the Wind*
Arrangement: Corchorus, lily, Chinese violet cress, paperplant, asparagus myriocladus
Vessel: Imitation porcelain plastic pot
Artist: Cai Zhongjuan

The corchorus is a deciduous dwarf shrub in the rose family and its flowering period is between April and May. With golden flowers and exquisite green leaves on gentle branches, it is ideal for making a slanting, horizontal, or pendent work of flower arrangement. In this work, the longest branch of the corchorus slants towards the right at a 45-degree angle. It serves as the first main branch that determines the slanting posture of this work. Other corchorus branches are obviously shorter than the first main branch, which are arranged on the left side or the rear of the work. The orange lilies are the focal flowers and the white Chinese violet cress is the supplement. The paperplants are arranged behind and beneath the focal area to enrich the frame and focal area itself. The asparagus myriocladus is used for embellishment.

3. Slanting

The first main branch is basically slanting, tilting between 15° and 75° to the vertical axis on the right or left (fig. 68).

Such a work, with sidewise branches and twigs, looks facile and graceful, presenting a dynamic or unyielding beauty (figs. 67 and 69 and see fig. 123 on page 115).

A slanting work often requires a sideway and curving branch or a dynamic but gentle branch as its first main branch, such as the plum blossom, Chinese flowering crabapple, magnolia, contorted willow, jujube, winter jasmine, golden bell, maple, pomegranate, hawthorn bush, pine, red-leaf cherry plum, phytolacca acinosa, barberry, rock cotoneaster, common aspidistra and areca palm. Other materials that can be used include the processed white willow, calla, and anthurium.

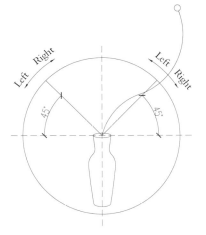

Fig. 68   The slanting posture.

Fig. 69   *Beauty in a Red Bathrobe*
Arrangement: Chinese flowering crabapple, Chinese herbaceous peony, sawara cypress
Vessel: Porcelain vase
Artist: Cai Zhongjuan

The longest branch of the Chinese flowering crabapple on the right of this work is the first main branch. It slants towards the right at the lower part and its upper part tilts towards the left at a 45-degree angle. A short branch of the Chinese flowering crabapple is added on the right side to enrich the frame. On the left side of the vase is arranged a shorter branch of the Chinese flowering crabapple that tilts towards the left at the lower part and towards the right at the upper part to echo the first main branch above and form a girth. On the left side of the Chinese flowering crabapple branch is also added a short branch to enrich the frame. The three Chinese herbaceous peonies are the focal flowers, and the sawara cypress serves both as a supplement and as embellishment. The whole work resembles a beauty after bath in a red bathrobe.

Fig. 70 *Meeting in the Golden Fall*
Arrangement: Reed catkin, sunflower, lotus seed pod, paperplant
Vessel: Porcelain vase
Artist: Cai Zhongjuan

The longest lotus seed pod serves as the first main branch, which extends naturally towards the left in a horizontal posture. The second main branch, the reed catkin, is arranged on the upper left corner of the vase, forming a contrast with the lotus seed pod. It should not exceed the first main branch in length. The third main branch is the sunflower, which reaches towards the right, balancing the first and second main branches. Beneath the three main branches are several branches of the same flowers. Varied in height, they are in picturesque disorder. At the bottom of this work are some short-branched paperplants.

Bottom on facing page
Fig. 73 *Light of Dawn*
Arrangement: Japanese maple, peony, paperplant
Vessel: Bamboo basket
Artist: Cai Zhongjuan

In ancient times, people regarded red, purple, and pink peonies as fine species, while white peonies were often undervalued. Fortunately, there were people who held a different view. They moved white peonies from remote mountain temples into their own gardens for cultivation. Bai Juyi (772–846), a well-known poet of Tang Dynasty, valued their effort and eulogized white peonies in poetry. Different from red, purple, and pink peonies, white peonies have their own advantages, one of which is that they make night less dark and are the first to greet the dawn. Basking in the morning sun, they look exquisite and noble. Later, white peonies have gradually become a rare peony species. This is a horizontal work arranged in a flower basket, with white peonies as the focal flowers, looking dignified and impressive.

Fig. 71 *Auspiciousness*
Arrangement: Houseleek, crassula hottentota, stapelia grandiflora, campfire plant, sedum morganianum, echeveria macdougallii
Vessel: Pottery pot
Artist: Ding Wenlin

This is an assorted Miniascape-Style work made of succulent plants. Dense as the plants are, they are varied in height and appropriately spaced, exhibiting a fine three-dimensional effect. The plants, which are mainly red, are decorated with red lanterns and other ornaments, presenting an atmosphere of auspiciousness. Such a work is ideal for festival celebrations.

4. Horizontal

The first main branch is basically horizontal, tilting about 15° above or below the horizontal axis (fig. 72).

Such a work looks either like a flying bird, graceful and unrestrained, or like a burbling brook, steady and dynamic (figs. 70, 71 and 73 and see fig. 61 on page 63).

A horizontal work requires a branch of line flowers with slightly upward bent twigs as the first main branch, such as the winter jasmine, primrose jasmine, golden bell, Chinese flowering crabapple, red-leaf cherry plum, snow willow, orange jessamine, snowrose, matrimony vine, weigela florida, and dendrobium. Other materials that can be used include the processed white willow, calla, and anthurium.

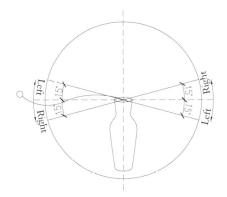

Fig. 72 The horizontal posture.

CHAPTER FIVE
Categories of Flower Arrangement

The rich variety of flower arrangement can be categorized from different perspectives. The categorization can be based on hisotrical times, floral vessels and techniques of expression. This chapter is also going to introduce the most major floral vessels of Chinese flower arrangement, with their origins, symbolic meaning, characerics as well as postures they usually take. The floral vessels can set off the flowers nicely. In Chinese flower arrangement, floral vessels are vital in artistic conception determination and creation.

On facing page
Fig. 74 *The Hidden Red Buds*
Arrangement: Chinese flowering crabapple, Chinese herbaceous peony, asparagus myriocladus
Vessel: Porcelain vase
Artist: Cai Zhongjuan

Arranged in a vase, this work is of a slanting posture. The three branches of the Chinese flowering crabapple form a main frame of asymmetric balance. The first main branch slants towards the right, the second main branch, which is about two thirds of the length of the first main branch, extends horizontally to the left, and the third main branch, which is about one third of the length of the first main branch, slants towards the right. The frame is further enriched by the short branches of the Chinese flowering crabapple arranged beneath the three main branches. The two white Chinese herbaceous peonies are in the focal area, one above and the other below, one on the left and the other on the right. The small red flowers on the branches of the Chinese flowering crabapple not only enrich the frame of this work, but also serve as the supplement flowers. The asparagus myriocladus strengthens the focal area and embellishes the whole work.

This work is mainly in green and white, looking elegant and refined. Dotted here and there by the buds of the Chinese flowering crabapple, it looks striking but not vulgar. This reminds the viewer of a poem composed by Yuan Haowen (1190–1257) to express his desire to preserve his own integrity and purity in disregard to the noisy craving for fame and profits of others. The poem goes: "The branches are turning greener with each of the passing day. Several small red buds are hidden deep among the leaves. Cherishing the fragrant stamens, they are reluctant to bloom, watching with dignity the peach flowers and plum blossoms striving noisily to gain the favor of the spring wind."

Fig. 75 *Reverie in Autumn*
Arrangement: Lindera obtusiloba, lily, chamomile, box
Vessel: Pottery pot
Artist: Xie Ming

Lindera obtusiloba has sparsely spaced branches and small fruits. Graceful and agile, it is used in this work as the frame. The Chinese box has dense and solid leaves and are arranged at the bottom to usher in the focal flowers. Although both of them are used as frame, they represent void and solidness respectively. Light on the top and weighty at the bottom, the overall composition looks comfortable. In the focal area, the lilies look solid while the chamomile void. They match each other perfectly. Although with fewer flowers, the whole work is hierarchically clear and appropriately spaced, showing charm and vividness.

1. Based on Historical Times

Like other forms of art, flower arrangement has changed along with the times. Chinese flower arrangement can be categorized into flower arrangement in ancient times and in modern times, each of which consists of several minor types.

Flower Arrangement in Ancient Times

Flower arrangement in ancient times (fig. 76) can be subcategorized into:

Flower arrangement for religious purposes. This kind of flower arrangement was mainly used as offerings in family halls for the Buddha, and thus it was also known as sacrificial flower arrangement. In this case, being solemn and dignified was the first concern, and the form of the work was not as important as the species of the flowers, which were often lotus flowers, as they were pure and clean.

Flower arrangement in royal palaces. Meticulous in structure and extravagant in outlook, this kind of flower arrangement was mainly used in royal palaces as decoration. The flowers used were large, colorful, magnificent, and luxuriant in foliage, such as the peony, Chinese herbaceous peony, camellia, plum, bamboo, and pine. Some works consisted of ten different kinds of flowers, suggesting perfection in every aspect. Some were homophonic, implying good fortune and auspiciousness.

Flower arrangement among common folks. This kind of flower arrangement occurred mostly in festivals or on ceremonious occasions, such as the Spring Festival, the Lantern Festival, the Dragon Boat Festival, the Magpie Festival, and the Mid-Autumn Festival. On these occasions, people often laid out pots of flowers decorated with spring couplets,

Fig. 76 *The Harmonious Colors of Spring*
Sun Kehong (1533–1611, Ming Dynasty)
Ink and color on silk
Height 131 cm × Width 63.4 cm
Palace Museum, Taibei

This work contains ten elements, such as pine, bamboo, plum blossom, cypress, camellia, narcissus, winter daphne, Chinese rose, sacred bamboo, and sesame stem. The flowers and leaves are luxuriant and dense, but in good order. The branches set off and echo each other perfectly.

paper cut-outs, knots, new-year pictures, lanterns, and scent bags to add to the happy festivities. Flower arrangement among common folks did not focus on presenting a particular outlook, but on creating an auspicious and joyous atmosphere. Therefore, most of the flowers used were fresh flowers with gorgeous colors. As it was made with pleasure, it was also known as Free-Style flower arrangement.

Flower arrangement by men of letters. Totally different from the previous three styles of flower arrangement, flower arrangement by men of letters was refined and elegant. It did not seek for ostentation and extravagance or for good fortune, but for the expression of the delights of life and the ideals and emotions of the flower

Fig 77 *Change of Seasons*
Arrangement: Dragon's claw willow, Japanese maple, strelitzia, sunflower, chamomile, leather leaf, lily, rice flower, field pennycress
Vessel: Decadent wooden peg
Artist: Wang Luchang

Floral vessels are not obligatory in flower arrangement. Self-made uniquely-shaped vessels are also possible. In this work, the flower arranger works on a grooved section of chinar and the fixing tools are placed right in the grooves. The willow branches in spring and the chamomile in autumn symbolize the change of seasons and the vitality of nature. Man, as part of nature, should live in harmony with it.

arranger. This kind of flower arrangement requires plain floral vessels and simple but elegant flowers such as the orchid, bamboo, plum blossom, and lily. The participation of a group of painters, calligraphers, poets, and literary writers in this trend had introduced into this form of art the law of beauty in form, an emphasis on proportional structures and the rhythm of balance. They instilled rich connotations into flower arrangement, making it culminate in the beauty of form and conception. It was this kind of flower arrangement that made the art of Chinese flower arrangement a specialized field of expertise.

Fig. 78 *Humbleness*
Arrangment: Chrysanthemum, Chinese flowering crabapple, Chinese St. John's wort fruit, freesia, azalea, sawara cypress, Chinese viburnum, decadent wood
Vessel: Pottery tray
Artist: Yuan Naifu

This is a work of floriculture design. The two pieces of decadent wood rise sheer from the level ground, constituting a tranquil valley, wide and far-reaching. Several bluish-green chrysanthemums are blooming one after another, like orchids in a deep valley, elegant and beautiful. Strings of red fruits are ripening in silence, like a man of great wisdom burying himself away in a remote mountain. This work connotes the spirit of humbleness. A man should have a mind as deep and broad as a valley; only with great concentration of mind can he, like a bird, soar into the vast sky with powerful wings.

Flower Arrangement in Modern Times

Flower arrangement in modern times consists of the following types:

Flower arrangement for ceremonies. This refers to flower arrangement on ceremonious occasions and for interpersonal interactions, such as flower baskets, bouquets, flower pots, garlands, festooned vehicles, and floral wreaths used in various public places or for festive ceremonies, weddings, guest-

welcoming, birthday celebrations, floral tributes, patient visits, and mourning. Flower arrangement of this kind usually has a fixed form, uses more flowers, and emphasizes the decorative, as well as the emotional effect. Since flower arrangement for ceremonies is highly commercial, it is also known as commercial flower arrangement.

Popular flower arrangement. This means that people arrange flowers for appreciation purposes. Such a work does not emphasize the composition, artistic conception, or connotations. It aims at decoration and adding vitality to the setting with the colors and fragrance of the flowers.

Artistic flower arrangement. This kind of flower arrangement, which emphasizes both form and artistic conception, is derived from the scholar's flower arrangement in ancient times. It varies in form, including impressionistic flower arrangement, Miniascape-Style flower arrangement, abstract flower arrangement, etc. It uses fewer flowers than flower arrangement for ceremonies, but is particular about the composition and rich in connotation. It was also known as creative flower arrangement.

Modern floriculture design. This can be understood as artistic flower arrangement in the broad sense. Works of this kind may or may not have floral vessels. They may be placed on a stand or table, or on the floor, and may be used to decorate a setting or the human body.

Floriculture design has the following features:

- Spatiality: Floricultural works can be placed in any spatial locations. Some can be on the floor or hanging; some can be fixed or mobile; some can be indoors or outdoors.
- Combinationality: Works of modern floriculture design are often large, formed by multiple individual works.
- Three-dimensionality: A work needs to be designed comprehensively and in great details. Some large-sized works allow viewers to enter them for appreciation.
- Originality: Modern floricultural works, in general, do not use regular floral vessels any longer. The floral vessel and the flowers are integrated into one and are designed and created by the designer himself. Therefore,

Fig. 79 *Far-Reaching Views from the Windows*
Arrangment: Decadent pear wood, tree section, sacred bamboo, oncidium, Chinese flowering crabapple fruit, pincushion flower, osmanthus, azalea, ceriman, orchid leaf, clematis, chrysanthemum, cornus officinalis fruit
Vessel: Picture frame and basin
Artist: Yuan Naifu

This is a Chinese-style floriculture design. The large decadent wood behind the picture frames is the long-range view, symblizing towering mountains. The decadent pear tree on the right side is the medium-range view, symbolizing ancient and well-known trees. The close-range view consists of flowers, grasses, and trees of different colors, which, set off by the giggling water and watergrass, display the artistic effect of Chinese-style courtyard views featuring frequent shifts of scenes and seeing the big within the small. Looking through the picture frame, the viewer may feel as if they were watching the wonders of nature and appreciating the fully blown wild flowers beyond a window, setting their imagniation free from the beautiful view this limited space can offer.

they boast unique characteristics and are seldom identical with others.
- Comprehensiveness: Modern floriculture design embodies the height of development of artistic flower arrangement. It integrates the art of flower arrangement with other forms of art (such as architectural art, decorative art, gardening art, stage art, window display art, industrial art, etc.) and techniques (such as composition, chromatology, literature, botany, material science, mechanics, engineering, optics, etc.). Because of this, large and medium-sized floriculture creations set a higher requirement for the flower arranger's knowledge reserve (fig. 79 and see fig. 77 on page 73 and fig. 78 on pages 74 and 75).

2. Based on Floral Vessels

Floral vessels can be used to hold water and keep the flowers fresh. Properly selected and used, they will have a great influence on a work. In the following, I will elaborate on the six major types of floral vessels based on their own symbolic meanings and characteristics. In addition, some new vessels often used in modern flower arrangement will also be introduced.

Vase Flowers

Origin: Vase flowers have their origin in the Northern and Southern Dynasties (420–581). As was said before, the bronze earthen jar in the 5th century, which was a container large in the middle and small at the mouth, was a vase-shaped floral vessel often found on Buddha stands in temples.

Vase flowers are the most characteristic and representative in traditional Chinese flower arrangement.

Symbolic meaning: Temples and big halls; high mountain ridges.

Characteristics:

- Vase flowers give prominence to the most beautiful part of the flowers in imitation of the technique of branch flower drawing in Chinese flower and bird painting, such as plum blossoms with sparse crosswise twigs, peonies with luxuriant foliage, elegant bamboo with thin and fresh leaves, grapes growing in close clusters, vigorous pines with luxuriant needles, wisterias with vines hanging to the ground. For vase flowers, the selection of the main flower is of particular importance, since, properly chosen, it will brighten up the whole work, or otherwise, make it a mess to look at.
- With sparse branches and fresh leaves, vase flowers are graceful, smooth, and natural.
- Vase flowers are the best if arranged impressionistically or without restraint.

Postures: upright, slanting, pendent, horizontal, and the combined types (fig. 80 and see fig. 4 on page 8 and fig. 74 on page 70).

Fig. 80 *Lingering Classic Elegance*
Arrangement: Lodgepole pine, chrysanthemum
Vessel: Porcelain vase
Artist: Cai Zhongjuan

Arranged in a vase, this work is of a semi-pendent posture. The blue vase goes well with the pine branches, creating a strong sense of classic elegance. Since both pines and autumn chrysanthemums are symbolic of faith and firmness, this work, though with fewer flowers, looks vigorous and forceful, dignified and impressive.

Pot Flowers

Origin: Pot flowers originated in the Northern and Southern Dynasties. In his poem *Apricot Flowers* the poet Yu Xin (513–581) recorded the scene of arranging the red apricot flowers into bronze plates, which were then placed on dinner tables to entertain guests. Similar scenes of flower arrangement were also mentioned in poems of that time.

It is clear that Chinese flower arrangement in its early stage consisted of two major forms: vase flowers and pot flowers.

Symbolic meaning: The earth, pools and ponds, the countryside, and courtyards.

Characteristics:

- Large at the mouth, the flower pot is the most ideal to display Miniascape-Style flower arrangement, such as lake ripples and sparkles, mountain views and rustic charm, a corner of the courtyard, pastoral scenes, and wild geese landing on the beach.
- The space for water in the pot creates fluidity, natural and congenial.
- Some works, furnished by decorative articles such as cobbles, stones, or artificial animals in the water areas, depict natural landscapes and add to the vitality of life.

Postures: Pot flowers are usually upright or slanting, though occasionally horizontal. The pendent posture is also possible if the pot is propped up high with a stand (figs. 81–83 and see fig. 75 on page 71).

Fig. 81 *Bamboo Setting Off the Water Clearer*
Arrangement: Bamboo, chamomile, dwarf lilyturf, asparagus myriocladus, Chinese St. John's wort fruit
Vessel: Imitation porcelain plastic pot
Artist: Cai Zhongjuan

This work portrays a corner in a courtyard: A grove of elegant bamboo grows alongside the pond, unique and charming. The blooming chamomile and the Chinese St. John's wort fruits on the ground imply the depth of autumn.

Fig. 82 *Flowers in Mid-Summer*
Arrangement: Calla, pomegranate branch, Chinese astilbe, anthurium leaf, New Zealand flax
Vessel: Pottery pot
Artist: Liang Shengfang

This work consists of a big flower pot and a small one, with pomegranate branches, New Zealand flax, and anthurium leaves as the frame, yellow callas as the focal flowers, and Chinese astilbe as the supplement. The two flower pots have the same flowers in them and the pomegranate branches on the right and left sides echo each other from bottom to top. Although arranged in two floral vessels, this work looks like one.

The pomegranate blooms in summer and its flowers are mostly red, though occasionally one can also find white, yellow, or pink pomegranate flowers. In this work, yellow pomegranate flowers are used, which coordinate with the yellow callas. Curly and with luxuriant leaves, pomegranate branches are often used as the frame of a flower arrangement.

Fig. 83 *Moonlight over the Lotus Pond*
Arrangement: Calamus, pond lily, lily pad
Vessel: Porcelain pot
Artist: Cai Zhongjuan

This is an upright work portraying water-front scenery, with the pot as the floral vessel. It consists of two groups of flowers. The taller flowers on the left are in the back and the lower flowers on the right are in the front. Though with few flowers, this work embodies all the six principles in composition.

This work is about a scene in mid-summer. White pond lilies are basked in the gentle moonlight, reminding the viewers of a well-known prose of the same name by Zhu Ziqing (1898–1948).

The pond lilies are either fully blown or in bud. Set off by layers of lily pads, they offer the viewers a real artistic treat.

Urn Flowers

Origin: The practice of arranging flowers in urns originated in the Tang Dynasty, as was recorded in *Nine Things in Flower Arrangement* by Luo Qiu. In the Tang Dynasty, people preferred to use big flowers like peonies in flower arrangement and the corresponding floral vessels were also big, such as urns and earthen jars, but urns in particular.

Symbolic meaning: Boldness and force.

Characteristics:

- Urns, which are shorter than vases and taller than pots, are solid and steady, setting off big flowers like peonies impressively.

- Urn flowers are mostly great in size, such as peonies, Chinese herbaceous peonies, lilies, day lilies, chrysanthemums, and camellias, which are furnished with branches of line flowers, such as Chinese flowering crabapples, plum blossoms, peach blossoms, apricot flowers, pines, cypresses, and sacred bamboo, to show the beauty of blocky flowers and line flowers in contrast. Sometimes, withered branches, wood sections, barks, and stones are mixed with fresh plants to show the natural scene of mutual generation.

Fig. 85 *Misty Rain in a Hill*
Arrangement: Peach tree, smoke tree, sawara cypress, lily, chamomile, anise, meadowsweet, ceriman
Vessel: Pottery urn
Artist: Cai Zhongjuan

This work, arranged in an urn, is of a slanting posture, focusing on portraying a scene in the hill. Although the branches of the peach tree are already dry and wilted, they effectively display the natural process of mutual generation. The flowers of the smoke tree make the whole work hazy and mysterious and increase its hierarchical changes. Small wild flowers are arranged in clusters to portray the mountain scenery and efforts are made to rid of any trace of the human touch.

- Urn flowers are usually placed on the floor. The small ones can be put on a short and stout stand, which is then placed on a table.

Postures: Urn flowers placed on the floor are mostly upright, solemn, and steady; smaller urn flowers placed on a table can be upright, slanting, or horizontal (figs. 84–85).

On facing page
Fig. 84 *Green Clouds Wafting out of Mountain Caves*
Arrangement: broadleaf mahonia, red-leaf cherry plum, pincushion flower, common goldenrod herb, asparagus myriocladus, sun spurge, bark
Vessel: Pottery urn
Artist: Cai Zhongjuan

Arranged in an urn, this work is of an upright posture. The two branches of broadleaf mahonia stand upright, towering into the sky. Their leaves are tabular and long, looking like green clouds wafting out of mountain caves, roving gracefully in the vast sky. The branches of red-leaf cherry plum on the lower right of the mountain rocks (made of barks) are slender and graceful, echoing the broadleaf mahonias above perfectly. The whole work resembles a well-proportioned Chinese painting, embodying a fine combination of inflexibility and yielding.

Fig. 87 *Beautiful and Gentle Branches*
Arrangement: Corchorus, Chinese rose, Chinese astilbe, leather leaf
Vessel: Porcelain bowl
Artist: Cai Zhongjuan

Arranged in a bowl, this work is of a slanting posture. The corchorus branches, which extend gracefully to the right and left, form the frame of the work in the shape of an asymmetric inverse triangle. The two Chinese roses in the center are the focal flowers, one taller and the other shorter. The Chinese astilbe is used for supplement and the leather leaves for ornaments. Since the bowl is normally deep in the center, the fixing tools in the bowl, such as the flower receptacle or floral foam, can be covered with small black pebbles.

On facing page
Fig. 86 *Happy and Content*
Arrangement: Calamus, eustoma, dendrobium, leather leaf
Vessel: Pottery bowl
Artist: Cai Zhongjuan

Arranged in a bowl, this work is of an upright posture. Such a work has its bottom concentrated in the center of the bowl and the flowers used often look noble and dignified. The flowers in this work are simple but elegant, giving expression to the philosophical idea of "cultivating one's moral character in peace and frugality."

Bowl Flowers

Origin: Bowl flowers emerged in the Five Dynasties and flourished in the Song Dynasty. Bowls and pots were originally household utensils, which were used as floral vessels later with changes in shape.

Symbolic meaning: Completeness, noble-mindedness, and elegance.

Characteristics:

- The bowl is large at the mouth and small at bottom. The setting tools are placed right in the center of the bottom. Flower arranging starts from the center and extends towards all sides.
- A typical work of bowl flowers in ancient time was semicircular on the top, which formed a circle with the bowl at the bottom, implying completeness. The flowers used were mostly big flowers like peonies and lotus flowers.
- Bowl flowers in later times became more lively and brisk in shape. The flowers, which can be noble and elegant or light and neat, concentrate at the bottom. The branches and foliage should not cover the bowl edge.

Postures: Bowl flowers can be upright and slanting, mainly upright (figs. 86–87).

Tube Flowers

Origin: Tube flowers have its origin in the Five Dynasties. The record about the Heavenly Abode of Flowers in the Song Dynasty shows that bamboo tube flowers were already popular at that time.

Fig. 88 *Song of Life*
Arrangement: Snowrose, Chinese rose, chrysanthemum, common goldenrod herb, leather leaf, asparagus myriocladus
Vessel: Bamboo tube
Artist: Cai Zhongjuan

With its powerfully winding branches and changing postures, the snowrose is ideal for arrangement in bamboo tubes. In this work, the snowrose branches on the right of the top opening are arranged in a pendent posture, echoing the semi-pendent snowrose branches on the left of the lower opening. Together, they constitute an organic whole. The Chinese roses in the top opening are gorgeously spirited while the yellow chrysanthemums at the lower opening are elegantly graceful, as if having weathered through the hardships of life.

Fig. 89 *Feeling Intoxicated*
Arrangement: Peony, weigela florida, calla, common aspidistra, meadowsweet, leather leaf
Vessel: Bamboo tube
Artist: Cai Zhongjuan

This work is arranged in a bamboo tube with two openings. In the top opening are arranged some branches of weigela florida, which extend horizontally towards the right. On the left are some short-branched weigela florida that echo the longer branches on the right. The two peonies are arranged in the focal area. In the lower opening are some common aspidistra leaves that slant towards the left, balancing the horizontal weigela florida branches in the top opening. The red callas are the focal flowers, which are supplemented by three or four leather leaves around them. Some meadowsweet are arranged near the focal flowers in the top and lower openings for embellishment.

Symbolic meaning: Noble-mindedness, elegance, and simplicity.

Characteristics:

- Tubes can be made of bamboo, wood, porcelain, etc., but the most common ones are bamboo tubes. A bamboo tube for a flower arrangement can have three kinds of openings: only one opening at the top, two openings including the lower one in the body of the tube, or more than two openings. The tube with two openings is the most commonly used. Flowers can be arranged in both openings or in the lower opening alone.
- The bamboo tube is thin and long, ideal for curved line composition. For example, one can use some woody materials as the frame of a work, such as Chinese gooseberry, oriental bittersweet, Chinese flowering crabapple, winter jasmine, barberry, snow willow, red-leaf cherry plum, snowrose, and Reeve's meadowsweet, and arrange some blocky flowers in the focal area, such as chrysanthemums, lilies, camellias, peonies, Chinese herbaceous peonies, and Chinese roses. The curves of the flowers and the straightness of the bamboo tube form a vivid contrast and the frame made of gentle branches and the thick and heavy focal flowers constitute balance.
- The bamboo tube is small at the mouth, so the flowers chosen should be small in number and light. Since bamboo is elegant and graceful, flowers that match this quality should be chosen, such as plum blossoms, orchids, and chrysanthemums.

Postures:

- Flowers arranged in a single-opening tube resemble that in a vase, so all postures, i.e. upright, slanting, pendent, horizontal, and the combined type, can be adopted.
- The postures of flowers arranged in a double-opening tube include: horizontal in the top opening and slanting in the lower opening (fig. 89), slanting in the top opening and horizontal in the lower opening, slanting in both openings (fig. 90), pendent in both openings (fig. 88), etc.

Fig. 90 *Smiling in the Spring Wind*
Arrangement: Wisteria, calla, Persian buttercup, lily, Chinese pink, leather leaf
Vessel: Bamboo tube
Artist: Cai Zhongjuan

The bended wisteria branches in the top and lower openings are all arranged in a slanting posture. The branches in the top opening bend towards the right, echoing from afar those in the lower opening that bend toward the left. The focal flowers in both openings are yellow, yellow callas in the top opening and yellow lilies in the lower opening. They are supplemented by orange Persian buttercups and white Chinese pinks, showing vigor and vitality. In this work, the wisteria buds, which are ready to burst, seem to smile in the spring wind and the Persian buttercups, lilies, and Chinese pinks are shining under the spring sunlight, presenting a spring scene of unparalleled beauty.

Fig. 92 *Flower Basket*
Li Song (Song Dynasty)
Ink and color on silk
Height 19.1 cm × Width 26.5 cm
Palace Museum, Beijing

Basket flowers in the Song Dynasty were mainly used in the imperial palace. The flowers used were steady and plump, extending towards all sides. They were huge in number and various in color. Such a work focuses on embellishment, ostentation, and extravagance.

On facing page
Fig. 91 *Tranquil Valley in a Small Hill*
Arrangement: Sacred bamboo, anise, lily, chamomile, meadowsweet, common aspidistra
Vessel: Bamboo basket
Artist: Cai Zhongjuan

This work is upright in posture, with the sacred bamboo branches and the common aspidistra leaves as the frame, the lilies as the focal flowers, and the anise, chamomile, and meadowsweets as the supplement and ornaments. Appropriate space has been left between the sacred bamboo branches and the common aspidistra leaves and between the lilies and other materials, thus giving prominence to the beauty of the umbrella-shaped branches of the sacred bamboo. At the bottom of the work is a section of decadent wood, which adds rustic interest to the work and balances the top and bottom.

Basket Flowers

Origin: Basket flowers originated in the Song Dynasty, as appeared in *Flower Basket*, a painting by Li Song (1190–1264) (fig. 92).

    Symbolic meaning: Auspiciousness, good fortune, and longevity.

    Characteristics:

- Basket flowers in the Song Dynasty were mostly used in the royal palaces. The flowers were gigantic and colorful, with luxuriant branches and leaves. The baskets were solemn-looking, highly decorative, and luxurious. Five kinds of flowers were often used, which were peonies, day lilies, magnolias, pomegranate flowers, and hollyhock flowers, implying the five blessings of longevity, wealth, health, virtue, and peaceful death. The flowers,

On facing page
Fig. 94 *Keeping the Flowers Awake*
Arrangement: Lindera obtusiloba, lily, chamomile, leather leaf, asparagus myriocladus
Vessel: Bamboo basket
Artist: Cai Zhongjuan

The flower baskets used in Chinese flower arrangement are mostly dark brown and varied in form. Since the basket in this work has a unique handle we have decided to arrange the flowers horizontally to reveal as much of the handle as possible. The branches and leaves of the lindera obtusiloba look like bright lamps shining over the delicate and charming lilies. This work takes its name from a poetic line in ancient China that shows the poet's tender care of the flowers. The dark red chamomile hidden among the branches and leaves are used as supplements, making the focal flowers and the lindera obtusiloba stand out.

Fig. 93 *Dragon Kept by the Charming Green*
Arrangement: Rubus rosifolius var. coronarius, iris, balloon flower, calla, common goldenrod herb
Vessel: Bamboo basket
Artist: Cai Zhongjuan

Arranged in a basket, this work is of a slanting posture. After being pruned, the branch of the rubus rosifolius var. coronarius looks exactly like a dragon ready to soar into the sky. It is the luxuriant green in spring that has kept him here. The Chinese flower arranger often tries to show the graceful beauty of some extremely fine branches by giving prominence to a branch. Meanwhile, to avoid monotony and abruptness, he also arranges beside the main branch another branch that bends towards the same direction as the main branch. This supporting branch can be taken from the same flower or from other kinds of flowers. The present work uses a wide-mouth basket as the vessel. The flowers are arranged mostly on the right side of the basket, while the left side is left empty, making the whole work natural and charming.

which were plump and extended to all sides, were arranged steadily, with no distinction between what is important and what is less important. Normally, the flowers were all below the bale handle of the basket. Flower arrangement of this kind focused not on symmetry, but on balance.

- Basket flowers in the Yuan and Ming dynasties had been instilled with the breath of scholars. Like vase flowers and pot flowers of that time, they were simple but refined, elegant but unrestrained. The focus of attention was not on symmetry in composition, but on artistic charm and cultural connotations.

- Modern basket flowers consist of two kinds: plump and asymmetric and artistic and non-asymmetric. They were used on ordinary and ceremonious occasions, respectively.

- Basket flowers are traditional flower arrangements with strong Chinese characteristics. In an arrangement, particular attention should be paid to the role of the basket handle as the frame of the whole work and to the proportionate organization of the space adjacent to the handle. The edge of the basket should be given careful consideration: some parts of it should be exposed to the air while other parts may be covered with flowers and leaves. Only in this way can the whole work look natural and vivid.

Postures: Basket flowers used on ceremonious occasions are mostly upright or horizontal in posture. Artistic flower baskets are mainly non-asymmetrically upright or slanting, though, occasionally, one can also find pendent and horizontal postures or postures of a combined type (figs. 93–94 and see fig. 91 on page 86).

Picture Frame Flowers

Origin: The picture frame as the background of a flower arrangement or as the floral vessel appears in modern times.

Symbolic meaning: Pictures in the frame and sceneries in the garden.

Characteristics:

- Specially-made picture frames can serve as floral vessels or as the background of flower arrangements.
- Picture frames come in various shapes, i.e. round, oval, square, rectangle, fan-shaped, hexagonal, octagonal, etc. They are often made of a double-layer wood board. The setting tools can be placed between the layers with a water-proof liner.
- The flowers should be carefully chosen and small in number. The composition should not be too sophisticated. The flower arranger can borrow from the techniques of Chinese flower and bird paintings, fan leaf paintings, and Chinese courtyard architecture.

Postures: Such works are mostly upright and slanting, but occasionally there are also some horizontal and pendent ones (figs. 95–97 and see fig. 103 on page 97 and fig. 108 on page 105).

Fig. 95 *Gentle Branches Swaying in the Wind*
Arrangement: Winged burning bush, pyracantha, sawara cypress, bark
Vessel: Wooden frame
Artist: Cai Zhongjuan

The circular picture frame in this work is an imitation of the moon gate design in Chinese gardening. It enables the flower arranger to focus on a more detailed display of a sight in a garden. In the lower right corner of this work are arranged a group of barks and flowers in good hierarchy, which focus on displaying the rustic views. In the upper left corner, a branch of the winged burning bush drifts down like a masterstroke that not only fills out the void but also invigorates the whole work. Though with few materials, this work looks like a Chinese painting that shows greatness in trivialness and uniqueness in mediocrity.

Fig. 96 *The Four Seasons*
Arrangement: Peony, vine with wild fruits on them, orchid leaf; lotus leaf, lotus seed pod, pond lily, styrax dasyanthus, chrysanthemum, oriental bittersweet, yellow cypress; plum blossom, small bamboo, lodgepole pine (from left to right)
Vessel: Wooden frame
Artist: Cai Zhongjuan

The artist uses four rectangular picture frames to portray the different scenes in the four seasons: the budding branches in spring, the fragrant lotus flowers in summer, the golden chrysanthemums in autumn, and the red plum blossoms in winter. Each of the frames makes a fine view like a three-dimensional picture and a soundless poem.

Fig. 97 *Natural and Unrestrained*
Arrangement: Golden bell, chrysanthemum, fragrant plantain lily flower, sawara cypress, balloon flower, red-leaf cherry plum, Chinese flowering crabapple
Vessel: Wooden frame
Artist: Chen Jingyi

This is a work in a picture frame with a horizontal posture. It portrays a scene of unrestrained freedom: the clouds in the sky are floating leisurely and the water in the river is giggling forward. This work can be hung on the wall for appreciation.

Fig. 98 *Whirling*
Arrangement: Strelitzia leaf, red willow, anthurium, oncidium
Vessel: Irregularly-shaped glass floral vessel
Artist: Xie Ming

This work is concise and modern. The wilted and curly strelitzia leaves expand the height of the floral vessel and constitute the upright central axis. In the middle upper part of the axis are arranged an anthurium flower, a cluster of oncidiums, and a branch of red willow, which exhibit vividly the three-dimensional effect. The composition embodies contrast in weight, abstractness, and rejuvenation, achiving a fine effect of appreciation.

Flower Arrangement in Irregularly–Shaped Floral Vessels

This is one of the forms of modern Chinese flower arrangement. The floral vessel is unlimited in shape, color, and texture, but the emphasis is on natural beauty and beauty in lines and artistic conception, which is realized sometimes by using some flower patterns or decorative techniques (fig. 98 and see fig. 105 on page 99).

Apart from the afore-mentioned eight kinds of flower arrangement, there are also combined types of flower arrangement using similar or different kinds of floral vessels, including mini flower arrangement (see fig. 107 on page 104).

Fig. 99 *Peach and Plum Branches Swaying in Spring Wind*
Arrangement: Red-leaf cherry plum, sawara cypress, common goldenrod herb, sweet William, Chinese ixora, bark
Vessel: Pottery pot
Artist: Cai Zhongjuan

This work is of a slanting posture. The focal area, which consists of barks, sawara cypress, and Chinese ixora, is solid and steady. The branches of the red-leaf cherry plum are dotted here and there, elegant and graceful, forming a vivid contrast with the flowers in the focal area. The relatively large expanse of water in the vessel makes the viewer feel as if this were a scene on the riverside, with cherry plum blossoms competing for beauty on a warm spring day.

3. Based on Techniques of Expression

Different techniques of expression in flower arrangement can result in different emphases in the creation process.

Miniascape-Style Flower Arrangement
Miniascape-Style Flower Arrangement presents part of nature in a vase or pot through artistic treatment. Such a work comes from nature but is above nature. A low-cut big pot is often used to present a specific corner in a courtyard, a pond-front scenery, or a hill corner (fig. 99 and see fig. 100 on page 94 and fig. 126 on pages 122 and 123).

Fig. 101 *Unyielding in the Cold*
Arrangement: Lodgepole pine, chrysanthemum, bark
Vessel: Wooden frame
Artist: Cai Zhongjuan

The two lodgepole pine branches in this work are arranged in the front and at the rear. The one in the front is solid while the one in the back is void. The two chrysanthemums face forward and sideways, representing solidness and void respectively. Though with few flowers, this work looks natural and hierarchical, embodying profound connotations. Pines and chrysanthemums are well-matched, since both are symbolic of strength of character and integrity. This work aims at encouraging the viewer with the unyielding characters of the flowers.

Impressionistic Flower Arrangement

This kind of flower arrangement does not focus on realistic scenery depictions, but on the expression of in-depth connotations. The flower arranger often expresses his individual wills, extols social virtues, or expounds philosophical truths by means of the floral vessel, flowers, composition, and color (fig. 101 and see fig. 127 on page 179).

Abstract Flower Arrangement

Flower arrangement of this kind is unlimited in composition. The flowers can be broken down for reorganization, so as to gain an unusual artistic effect through the use of various new techniques of expression. Such works can focus on the decorative effect or on the artistic conception, or on both (see fig. 128 on page 179).

On facing page
Fig. 100 *Voice of Spring in a Secluded Valley*
Arrangement: Elm, iris, bell flower, common goldenrod herb, sweet William, blue throatwort, sun spurge, section of wood
Vessel: Pottery pot
Artist: Cai Zhongjuan

This work transplants the scene of nature into a flower pot for appreciation, making you feel as if you were in a secluded valley listening to the incoming footsteps of spring. The dark-red flower pot resembles the earth or a corner of a hill, in which the tender leaves of the elm begin to burst out. Beneath the elm are wild flowers and grasses blown back to life by the gentle spring wind. The pink bell flowers, common goldenrod herbs, and the blue irises beside herald the advent of spring, filling the valley with their pleasant smell and vigor.

The little elm on the left, with few twigs and tiny leaves, matches perfectly with the irises on the right, which have fat leaves and robust flowers. The pink bell flowers under the elm echo the sweet William under the irises at a distance, and so do the blue throatwort flowers and the blue irises. For the best natural effect, there is no need for more colors. The wood sections and the barks on the ground add to the flavor of nature.

CHAPTER SIX
Commonly-Used Flowers and Their Selection

The materials used in Chinese flower arrangement are many and diversified, including woody plants, herbaceous plants, water plants, roots, stems, flowers, leaves, fruits of plants, etc. Virtually, all plants with viewing values and free from poison and harm can be used. This chapter will introduce some commonly used flowers and how to select the flowers.

Fig. 103 *The Demeanor of a Refined Gentleman*
Arrangement: Cymbidium, orchid leaf
Vessel: Wooden frame
Artist: Cai Zhongjuan

The fan-shaped picture frame can be taken as the window frame of a long corridor in Chinese gardens or in a traditional Chinese fan leaf painting. The cluster of cymbidium and orchid leaves in this work is simple and elegant, graceful and natural, reminding the viewer of a refined gentleman.

On facing page
Fig. 102 *Elegance in Simplicity*
Arrangement: Golden bell, orchid leaf, lily, chamomile, anthurium leaf
Vessel: Porcelain vase
Artist: Cai Zhongjuan

In Chinese flower arrangement, it is traditionally required that the bottom of a work be concentrated at one point, as if all the flowers grew out of the same root, and the branches fan out naturally in diverse postures. In this work, the branches and leaves are sparsely distributed, natural and graceful, while the flowers are placed closely together in the center, heavy and steady. The whole work, fanning out on the top and concentrated at the bottom, is natural and unrestrained.

1. How to Choose Flowers

Flowers are the main ingredients in flower arrangement. Whether they are properly chosen affects a work significantly. In choosing flowers, one must bear in mind the following points.

Selection based on the theme of the work. The shape and color of the flower and the message it carries must be able to intensify the expression of the theme.

Selection based on a combination of different shapes of flowers. The line flower, such as the white willow, contorted willow, red twig dogwood, winter jasmine, snow willow, golden bell, orange jessamine, calamus, scirpus tabernaemontani, etc. is often used as the frame flower. The blocky flower, such as the lily, peony, Chinese herbaceous peony, Chinese rose, and sunflower, is often used as the focal flower. The dot-shaped flower, such as the common goldenrod herb, gmelin's sea lavender herb, statice, freesia, chamomile, Chinese pink, meadowsweet, Chinese St. John's wort fruit, etc., is often used as the supplement flower. The combinational use of different shapes of flowers in different parts of the work makes the work natural and harmonious.

Selection based on the human qualities of the flowers. Since flowers grow in different natural conditions and are different in their ability to resist environmental changes, people bestow them with different qualities, such as the pine for unyieldingness and nobleness, the plum blossom for firmness and detachment, the bamboo for uprightness and loftiness, the chrysanthemum for bravery in adversities, the orchid for being extraordinarily refined, the lotus flower for purity, etc. In the eyes of the ancient Chinese, the plum blossom, orchid, bamboo, and chrysanthemum were gentlemen among flowers and the pine, bamboo, and plum blossom were the three companions in winter. Therefore, generally, the pine and plum blossom should go with the chrysanthemum, camellia, and dark-colored Chinese rose that are solemn-

Fig. 104 *Round Moon and Beautiful Flowers*
Arrangement: White willow, peony, peony leaf
Vessel: Pottery vase
Artist: Cai Zhongjuan

The two groups of white willow branches form an opened circle, symbolizing the moon. A cluster of peonies with different colors are luxuriant and voluptuous, symbolizing auspiciousness, riches and honor. The whole work carries the message of fineness and perfection.

Fig. 105 *Eternal Love*
Arrangement: Chinese rose, osier, white lace flower
Vessel: Irregularly-shaped floral vessel
Artist: Xie Ming

Flowers could have been arranged at the mouths of this group of irregularly-shaped white porcelain vases. However, the artist has broken the convention by arranging two groups of flowers on the floral foam sticked to the deep-set vase bellies. The flowers face each other charmingly, looking like a loving couple pledging eternal love to each other. The whole work is original in conception, graceful in shape, harmonious in color, and profound in connotation.

looking, the bamboo with the chrysanthemum, orchid, and plum blossom, and the chrysanthemum with the pine, cypress, and pyracantha.

Selection based on the ecological behaviors of the flowers. Due to different growing environments, different flowers have different ecological behaviors. For example, the plum blossom is resistant to cold, the plantain loves warmth, the pine and fir are draught tolerant, and the lotus flower is fond of wetness. If the work is to depict mountain scenery, then xerophilous plants such as the pine, cypress, poplar, willow, camellia, azalea, peony, Chinese herbaceous peony, winter jasmine, and pyracantha can be put together. If it is a waterscape, then water plants can be chosen, such as the calamus, scirpus tabernaemontani, lotus flower, pond lily, willow herb, iris, and reed catkins.

Selection based on the customs of gift-giving. Different flowers have different languages and are used to express different emotions and wishes (fig. 106). For example, on Valentine's Day, roses are chosen as they symbolize love; on Mother's Day, carnations are the best choice as they represent holiness and elegance; on Father's Day, sunflowers are preferred as they mean silent paternal love; on the Day for the Aged, strelitzias are chosen as they symbolize longevity.

2. Commonly-Used Flowers

This section presents a table of those commonly used flowers, with their scientific names, common names and the periods of appreciation.

Fig. 106 *Ascending Another Story of a Building*
Arrangement: White willow, chrysanthemum, lily, coral, paperplant, asparagus myriocladus
Vessel: Bamboo tube
Artist: Cai Zhongjuan

The two groups of white willow branches are in an ascending spiral, as if scaling heights. Although the bamboo tube has only two stories, it creates an endless space for the willow branches to move upward.

◆ Scientific Name ★ Period of Appreciation ◇ Common Name

1	◆ Prunus mume ★ Jan.–Apr. ◇ Plum blossom	2	◆ Camellia japonica ★ Jan.–Mar. ◇ Camellia
3	◆ Magnolia denudata ★ Mar.–Apr. ◇ Magnolia	4	◆ Chaenomeles lagenaria ★ Mar.–Apr. ◇ Flowering quince
5	◆ Malus spectabilis ★ Apr.–May ◇ Chinese flowering crabapple	6	◆ Paeonia Suffruticosa ★ Apr.–May ◇ Peony
7	◆ Paeonia lactiflora ★ Spring ◇ Chinese herbaceous peony	8	◆ Prunus persica ★ Mar.–Apr. ◇ Peach flower
9	◆ Prunus cerasifera ★ All year round ◇ Red-leaf cherry plum	10	◆ Punica granatum ★ Flower: May–Aug. ★ Fruit: May–Oct. ◇ Pomegranate
11	◆ Rhododendron ★ Spring and summer ◇ Azalea	12	◆ Salix matsudana f. tortuosa ★ All year round ◇ Contorted willow
13	◆ Ziziphus jujuba ★ All year round ◇ Jujube	14	◆ Pyracantha fortuneana ★ Autumn and winter ◇ Pyracantha
15	◆ Berberis thunbergii ★ All year round ◇ Barberry	16	◆ Cornus alba ★ All year round ◇ Red twig dogwood
17	◆ Cotoneaster horizontalis ★ All year round ◇ Rock cotoneaster	18	◆ Nandina domestica ★ All year round ◇ Sacred bamboo
19	◆ Acer palmatum ★ All year round ◇ Japanese maple	20	◆ Wisteria sinensis ★ Apr.–May ◇ Wisteria

21	◆ Jasminum nudiflorum ★ Feb.–Mar. ◇ Winter jasmine	22	◆ Forsythia suspensa ★ Feb.–May ◇ Golden bell
23	◆ Lycium chinense ★ Autumn ◇ Matrimony vine	24	◆ Salix leucopithecia ★ Winter and spring ◇ White willow
25	◆ Actinidia chinensis ★ All year round ◇ Chinese gooseberry	26	◆ Serissa serissoides ★ Branch: All year round ★ Flower: Jun.–Sep. ◇ Snowrose
27	◆ Murraya paniculata ★ Autumn ◇ Orange jessamine	28	◆ Fontanesia fortunei ★ Spring ◇ Snow willow
29	◆ Mahonia bealei ★ All year round ◇ Broadleaf mahonia	30	◆ Fatsia japonica ★ All year round ◇ Paperplant
31	◆ Monstera deliciosa ★ All year round ◇ Ceriman	32	◆ Pinus thunbergii ★ All year round ◇ Lodgepole pine
33	◆ Osmanthus fragrans ★ Branch: All year round ★ Flower: Autumn ◇ Sweet osmanthus	34	◆ Hypericum monogynum ★ After Jul. ◇ Chinese St. John's wort fruit
35	◆ Rosa chinensis ★ All year round ◇ Chinese rose	36	◆ Lilium ★ All year round ◇ Lily
37	◆ Iris tectorum ★ Spring ◇ Iris	38	◆ Zantedeschia aethiopica ★ Winter and spring ◇ Calla
39	◆ Strelitzia reginae ★ All year round ◇ Strelitzia	40	◆ Dendrobium nobile ★ All year round ◇ Dendrobium

41	◆ Phalaenopsis amabilis
	★ Winter and spring
	◇ Moth orchid

42	◆ Dendranthema morifolium
	★ All year round
	◇ Chrysanthemum

43	◆ Nelumbo nucifera
	★ Summer and autumn
	◇ Lotus

44	◆ Nymphaea tetragona
	★ Summer
	◇ Pond lily

45	◆ Anthurium scherzerianum
	★ All year round
	◇ Anthurium

46	◆ Dianthus barbatus
	★ Winter and spring
	◇ Sweet William

47	◆ Dianthus Chinensis
	★ Spring
	◇ Chinese pink

48	◆ Solidago canadensis
	★ All year round
	◇ Common goldenrod herb

49	◆ Limonium
	★ All year round
	◇ Gmelin's sea lavender herb

50	◆ Helianthus angustifolius
	★ Summer and autumn
	◇ Sunflower

51	◆ Protea cynaroides
	★ Winter and spring
	◇ King protea

52	◆ Leucospermum nutans
	★ All year round
	◇ Pincushion flower

53	◆ Bambusoideae
	★ All year round
	◇ Bamboo

54	◆ Miscanthus sacchariflorus
	★ Autumn and winter
	◇ Amur silver grass

55	◆ Acorus calamus
	★ Spring, summer and autumn
	◇ Calamus

56	◆ Scirpus tabernaemontani
	★ Spring, summer and autumn
	◇ Scirpus tabernaemontani

57	◆ Asparagus myriocladus
	★ All year round
	◇ Asparagus myriocladus

58	◆ Ophiopogon japonicus
	★ All year round
	◇ Dwarf lilyturf

59	◆ Aspidistra elatior Blume
	★ All year round
	◇ Common aspidistra

60	◆ Arachniodes adiantiformis
	★ All year round
	◇ Leather leaf

CHAPTER SEVEN
Floral Vessels and Tools

A lot of floral vessels are used for flower arrangement. In a good flower arrangement, the floral vessel, flowers, and the flower pattern are an organic whole. Therefore, finding a good floral vessel is decisive in the flower arranging process.

There are also many tools used in flower arrangement. Apart from the commonly-used ones, there are also some supplementary tools, each of which functions in its own way.

On facing page
Fig. 107 *A World in Miniature*
Arrangement: Periwinkle, Japanese maple, Buddhist pine, chamomile, azalea, ivy
Vessel: Mini-vases and pots
Artist: Cai Zhongjuan

This is a set of mini flower arrangements placed on a redwood antique-and-curio shelf. Each work is a little more than 10 centimeters in height and can be held by hand for appreciation. The shelf, about 90 centimeters in height, can be placed on a stand or table. Since it is small, the flowers can be arranged in a slanting, pendant, or horizontal posture and the materials used, such as flowers, grasses, branches, and leaves, should also be small. Though with few flowers, this work still follows the art of composition in displaying the unique artistic effect.

Fig. 108 *Drunken Moon and Floating Clouds*
Arrangement: Amur silver grass, chrysanthemum, leather leaf, bark
Vessel: Wooden frame
Artist: Cai Zhongjuan

The circular picture frame is often used to portray scenes under moonlight. Amur silver grass is a very beautiful Gramineae plant and its inflorescence is light and airy, often known figuratively as floating clouds. This work expresses the intoxicating charm of white flowers floating under the bright autumn moon.

1. Floral Vessels

Six floral vessels are common in Chinese flower arrangement, which are the vase, pot, urn, bowl, tube, and basket. Two others have emerged in modern times: the picture frame and the irregularly-shaped floral vessel.

The Vase
The vase is the most commonly used container for Chinese flower arrangement. It comes in different shapes, i.e. tube-shaped, beer-belly shaped, ball-shaped, square-mouthed, etc. It is made of porcelain, bamboo, metal, stone, or imitation porcelain (fig. 109).

Vases

Fig. 109   Vases

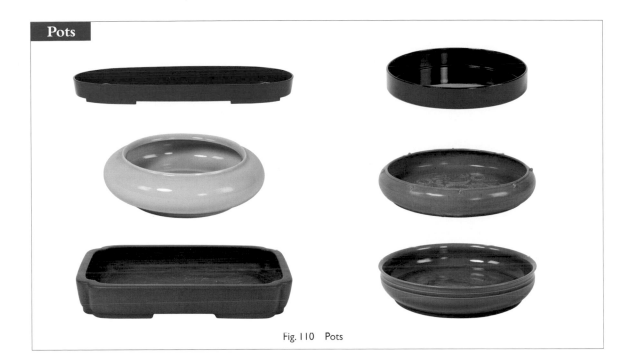

Fig. 110   Pots

The Pot

The flower pot is broad at the mouth and shallow. It is round, oval, square, rectangle, or lotus-leaf shaped. It is made of porcelain, copper, stone, imitation porcelain, etc. (fig. 110).

The Urn

The urn is a large-size, plain, and heavy container. It is taller than the pot and lower than the vase. It is mainly made of porcelain, and occasionally of stone or glass fiber reinforced plastic (fig. 111).

Fig. 111   Urns

Fig. 112   Bowls

The Bowl

The bowl is large at the mouth and small at the bottom. It is mostly round and made of porcelain, lacquer wood, and imitation porcelain (fig. 112).

The Basket

The basket is a floral vessel with a bale handle. It is round, oval, square, or boat-shaped. It is mainly woven with slices of bamboo, vines, or willow branches. Some baskets are also made of porcelain, glass, or metals. Basket flowers can be presented as a gift or simply be an object for appreciation (fig. 113).

Baskets

Fig. 113   Baskets

The Tube
The tube used in flower arrangement may have one opening, two openings, or multiple openings. It is mostly made of tortoise-shell bamboo, and occasionally of porcelain or imitation porcelain (fig. 114).

Tubes

Fig. 114   Tubes

The Picture Frame
The picture frame as a floral vessel appears in modern times. It can produce excellent framed sceneries and see-through effects. It comes in various shapes: round, oval, square, rectangle, fan-shaped, hexagonal, octagonal, etc. The picture frame is often made of double-layer wood boards, acrylic materials, or aluminum sheets. Water-holding containers and setting tools are often placed between the layers (fig. 115).

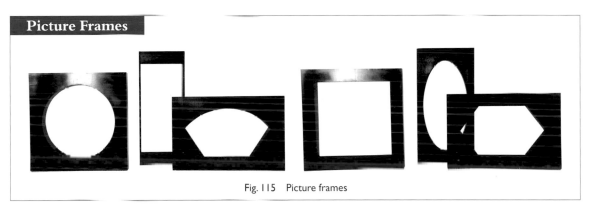

Picture Frames

Fig. 115   Picture frames

The Irregularly-Shaped Floral Vessel
The irregularly shaped floral vessel is derived from ancient floral vessels through transfiguration and abstraction. It is powerful in artistic expression and rich in composition, color, and texture (fig. 116).

Irregularly-Shaped Floral Vessels

Fig. 116   Irregularly-shaped floral vessels

2. Stands and Decorative Items

Some works of flower arrangement are equipped with a stand or decorative items to increase the aesthetic interest or set off the theme and artistic conception.

The stand is of diverse shapes and made of rosewood, imitation rosewood, boxwood, bamboo, tree roots, porcelain, etc. (fig. 117).

The decorative items are made of different materials in the form of birds and beasts, human figures, or handicrafts.

Stands

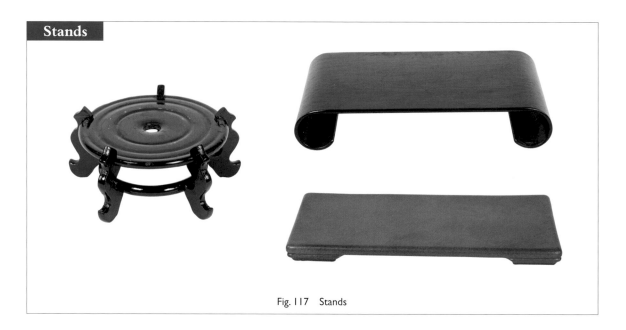

Fig. 117   Stands

3. Processing Tools

Below are those processing tools commonly-used in Chinese flower arrangement (fig. 118).

The scissors. The home-use clippers can be used to cut ordinary flower leaves, but the pruning shears should be used for cutting branches.

The pliers. Use the lock wrench to cut thick aluminum wires and the long flat nose pliers to cut fine aluminum wires.

The utility knife. It is mainly used to cut the floral foam.

The chest saw. It is used to cut thick branches, wood sections, or bamboos.

The metal wire. This mainly includes the copper wire, aluminum wire, and iron wire. The commonly-used wire gauges range from 20 to 30. The bigger the gauge is, the finer the wire is, and the smaller the gauge is, the thicker it is. The colors of the wire are green or brown, depending on the branch colors.

Processing Tools

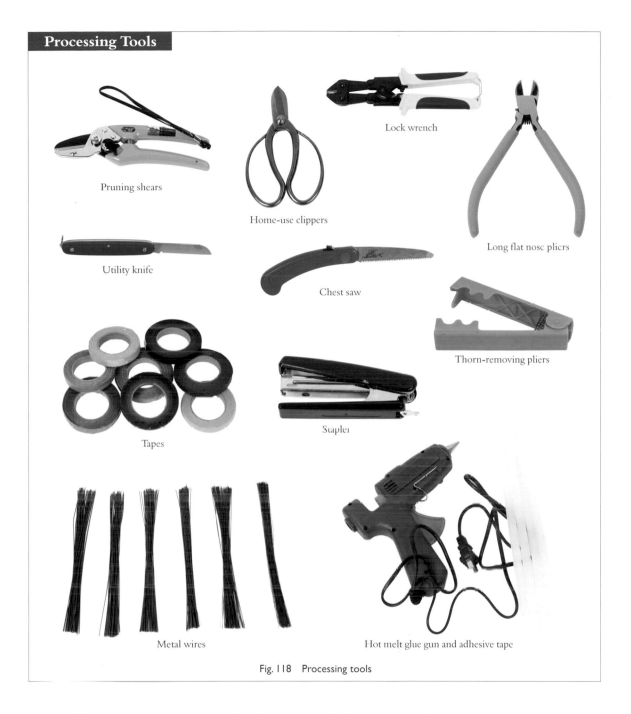

Pruning shears

Home-use clippers

Lock wrench

Long flat nose pliers

Utility knife

Chest saw

Thorn-removing pliers

Tapes

Stapler

Metal wires

Hot melt glue gun and adhesive tape

Fig. 118   Processing tools

The tape. The tape is often dark green, light green, or brown. It is used to bind up the branches wrapped with iron wires.

The stapler. It is used for fixing the leaves that curl up.

The thorn-removing pliers. They are used to remove the thorns on the branches of the Chinese rose.

The hot melt glue gun and adhesive tape. In artificial flower arrangement, they are used to secure the floral foam and the floral vessel, the flowers and floral foam, and artificial flower treatment.

4. Fixing Tools and Their Uses

Chinese flower arrangement requires a lot of fixing tools. In the following, I will introduce some commonly-used tools and the methods of using them.

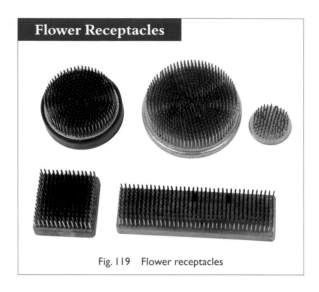

Fig. 119   Flower receptacles

The Flower Receptacle

The flower receptacle, also known vividly as the Hill of Swords, consists of copper needles on a lead or aluminum-alloy base (fig. 119), which do not rust in water and can stabilize the flowers. A high-quality flower receptacle has long and dense cooper needles and a lead base of appropriate thickness. Some lead bases are rimmed with a rubber band that makes the bases skid-proof and protects the floral vessel.

When the flower receptacle is used for arranging herbaceous plants or woody plants loose in texture, the plants are usually made flat at the bottom, since an increased interface area will help stabilize the plants. If the woody plants are hard, the bottom should be made diagonal. If the plants are too slim, they can be placed into a thick stem, which is then secured by the flower receptacle, or they can be bundled up for arrangement.

Some woody plants are heavy and may prostrate if arranged on one side. In this case, another flower receptacle can be placed upside down on the other side opposite to the direction of the prostration to gain balance.

The flower receptacle can be used in such floral vessels as flower pots, big-mouth vases, bamboo tubes, bowls, urns, baskets, and picture frames.

The Bracket at the Mouth of the Floral Vessel

In order to narrow the space at the mouth of the floral vessel and fix the flowers and the angle of flower arrangement, one can make a cross-shaped, pound-sign-shaped, or Y-shaped bracket to space the floral vessel mouth (fig. 120). The bracket can be made secure by leaning it closely against the wall of the floral vessel or by tying it to an upright branch with a thread, rope, or rubber band.

The bracket can be used to fix flowers in various floral vessels.

Clusters of Straw and Thin Bamboo Sticks As the Fixing Tool

A cluster of straw or thin bamboo sticks tied closely together can be placed inside the vase or tube to fix the flowers. The straw must be steamed or

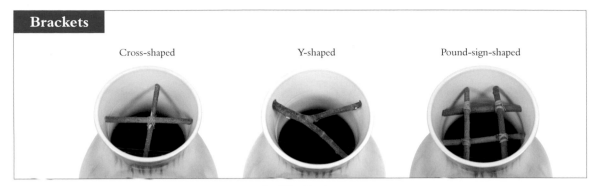

Brackets

Cross-shaped Y-shaped Pound-sign-shaped

Fig. 120 Brackets

boiled to avoid going moldy.

This method can be used in fixing flowers in vases or bamboo tubes.

The Metal Wire Ball

Form the metal wires that are not apt to rust (such as copper or aluminum wires) into a ball and put it into the vase. The flowers can be inserted into the cracks in the ball for securement. This method is good for vase flower arrangement.

Floral Foam

Floral foam as a fixing tool in flower arrangement appeared in the 1970s and 1980s. Made of Bakelite, it is a one-time flower fixing tool. As floral foam is ideal for multi-angle flower arrangement and easy for transportation, it is extensively used today.

Floral Foam

Wet floral foam

Dry floral foam

Fig. 121 Floral foam

There are two kinds of floral foam: green wet floral foam and light cream-colored dry floral foam. The former, which must be fully soaked with water before use, is ideal for fresh flower arrangement. The latter, which does not require immersion in water, is used for the arrangement of dry flowers or artificial flowers (fig. 121).

Floral Foam Combined with the Bracket or Barbed Wire

The branches of some woody plants used in large-sized works of flower arrangement, such as urn flowers, are heavy. In order to secure the angle of branches and prevent the floral foam from becoming loose, the floral foam can be placed at the bottom of the floral vessel, and covered with a layer of brackets or with barbed wire. Also a double-layer bracket can be placed at the top and bottom of the floral vessel and the floral foam is fixed in the middle.

CHAPTER EIGHT
Manufacturing Techniques

Chinese flower arrangement is a practice-based art, which requires the flower arranger to have both profound artistic cultivation and much practice. Only when one is skillful in composition and excels in using setting tools of different kinds can he gradually become experienced in flower arrangement.

On facing page
Fig. 122 *Fragrance in Morning Breeze*
Arrangement: Alocasia rhizome, lily, common goldenrod herb, asparagus myriocladus, vine
Vessel: Porcelain vase
Artist: Cai Zhongjuan

The branches and leaves on the upper left side bend towards the right and the vines on the lower right side bend towards the left. They echo each other from top to bottom, forming an organic whole. The branches of the alocasia rhizome serve as the frame, the lilies as the focal flowers, the common goldenrod herbs as the supplements, and the asparagus myriocladus as the ornaments. The lilies are in full bloom and its fragrance spreads far and wide with the swaying branches of the alocasia rhizome.

Fig.123 *Flowers Smiling in Spring*
Arrangement: Waxy-leaf privet, peony, paperplant
Vessel: Wooden frame
Artist: Cai Zhongjuan

A picture frame work often portrays part of a natural scene. This work depicts a corner of a garden in spring. A group of waxy-leaf privet branches with tender leaves are arranged slantingly on the upper left of the picture frame and a group of purple and red peonies on the lower right of the frame. Elegant and beautiful, they seem to be smiling in the intoxicating spring wind. This work embodies all the principles of composition.

1. Flower Treatment

Flower treatment is the first step in flower arrangement, the quality of which directly affects the beauty of the work.

Pruning the Woody Plants

In Chinese flower arrangement, the redundant branches, including those that are unnecessary, overlapping, parallel, intersecting, damaged, sick, and wilted, must be removed to bring out the most beautiful branches.

When the side branches are being cut, the pruning wounds should cling to the main branch, no short branches should be left, and the incision should be natural and smooth. The branches should vary in height at the top, instead of being the same height.

Bending the Branches

Branches that are not too thick and hard can be gradually bent at the right places section by section with both hands. A shallow cut on the back of the branch is needed for bending thick and hard branches. If the branch is thick and the cut is deep, a wooden peg can be inserted into the cut for fixing.

Bending the Branches

B ranches that are not too thick and hard can be gradually bent at the right places section by section with both hands.

A shallow cut on the back of the branch is needed for bending thick and hard branches.

If the branch is thick and the cut is deep, a wooden peg can be inserted into the cut for fixing.

Branch Decoration

Some epiphytes such as mosses and lichens can be pasted on the surfaces of some thick branches to add to their vigor and vitality. If the pruning wound is too conspicuous, one can use mud or paste some barks, mosses, or lichens to cover it up.

Bending the Leaves

To adjust the camber of a leaf, such as that of the common aspidistra and iris, one can paste a 20 to 22 gauge iron wire with a cellulose tape at the central vein on the back of the leave.

Bending the Leaves

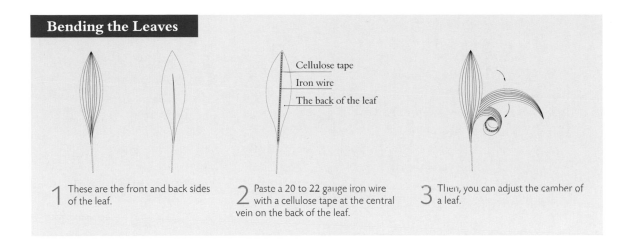

Cellulose tape
Iron wire
The back of the leaf

1 These are the front and back sides of the leaf.

2 Paste a 20 to 22 gauge iron wire with a cellulose tape at the central vein on the back of the leaf.

3 Then, you can adjust the camber of a leaf.

Pulling through the Stem with a Metal Wire

Pull a 22 to 24 gauge metal wire ranging through the hollow or loose stem of a flower, such as the calla, pond lily, Persian buttercup, etc., to adjust the camber of the stem without damaging its exterior condition.

Pulling through the Stem with a Metal Wire

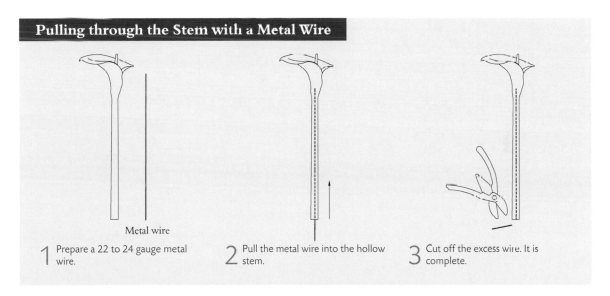

Metal wire

1 Prepare a 22 to 24 gauge metal wire.

2 Pull the metal wire into the hollow stem.

3 Cut off the excess wire. It is complete.

Tips

1. Bending the Canes

Dry canes bought from the market can be soaked in water first before bending them into the required forms for use after they dry.

2. Removing the Sepals of the Pond Lily

The pond lily blooms only in the day time. However, its sepals can be removed for around-the-clock appreciation.

2. Procedures of Flower Arrangement

As soon as the floral vessel, flowers, and fixing tools are ready, one can start arranging the flowers. Beginners can follow four steps to finish the work: determining the frame flowers, deciding on the focal flower, adding supplement flowers, and making the decoration. In the beginning, they can follow these steps closely, but after they have become proficient with flower arrangement, these steps can be followed alternately. Since compositions in flower arrangement vary, I will illustrate the four procedures one by one (fig. 124).

Determining the Frame Flowers

Three things must be determined one by one: the basic posture of the work (either upright, slanting, horizontal, or pendent), the proportion between the flowers and the floral vessel, and the focal flowers to be used.

The frame flowers are often line flowers, such as the white willow, contorted willow, snow willow, red twig dogwood, calamus, bamboo, scirpus tabernaemontani, etc.

Deciding on the Focal Flower

The focal flower of a work, which lies in the center of gravity of the work, is an important part of the work. It is located at the place one third of the height of the main branch.

The focal flower is often a blocky flower, such as the peony, Chinese herbaceous peony, chrysanthemum, lily, pond lily, Chinese rose, king protea, etc.

Adding Supplement Flowers

Supplement flowers link the frame flowers and focal flower. They are often located adjacent to the focal flower, about a half of the frame flowers in height or breadth. They add to the colors, layers, and dynamism of the work and help form a three-dimensional effect.

Supplement flowers are often small flowers and fruits, such as the chamomile, common goldenrod herb, gmelin's sea lavender herb, lilac, sweet William, Chinese St. John's wort fruit, etc.

Making the Decoration

After the above procedures are completed, grasses and small leaves and flowers should be used to cover up the fixing tools and other human traces for a natural effect.

Meanwhile, the whole work should be examined one last time, with unnecessary flowers and leaves removed, and necessary ones added.

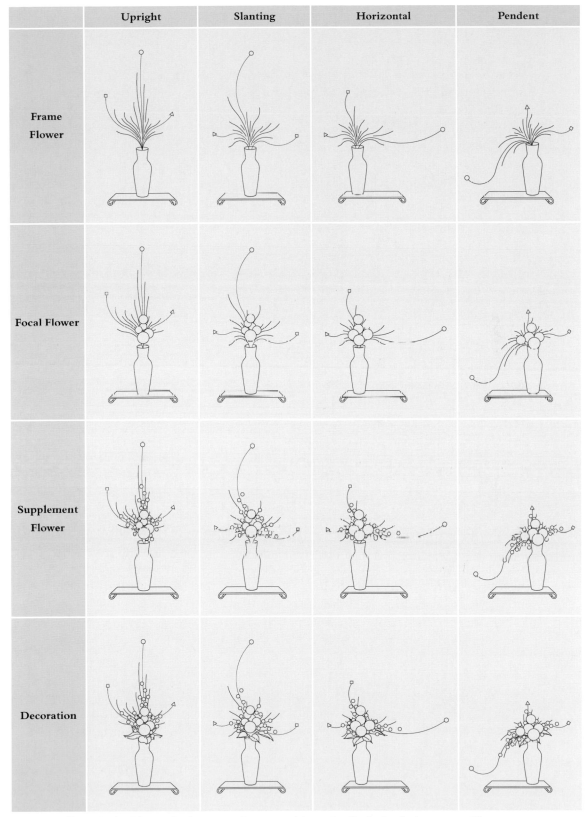

	Upright	Slanting	Horizontal	Pendent
Frame Flower				
Focal Flower				
Supplement Flower				
Decoration				

Fig. 124   Different kinds of frames, focal areas, supplements, and decoration for the four basic postures of flower arrangement.

3. Display and Positioning

After the completion of the whole work, an appropriate setting should be chosen for display, which, if well done, will provide the crowning touch to the work.

Being Coordinated with the Setting

First, the size of the work must match that of the setting. A big work in a small setting is depressive, and a small work in a big setting is petty. A long and narrow setting requires an upright work and a low and wide setting a slanting or horizontal work (fig. 125).

Second, the sophistication of the work must match the function of the room in which the work is placed. Works placed in the living room or lobby should be plump and gorgeous, those in the bedroom should be exquisite and warm, those

Fig. 125 *Autumn of Yangzhou*
Arrangement: Sacred bamboo, cockscomb, chrysanthemum, lily, Chinese pink, Chinese rose, Chinese juniper, osmanthus, paperplant, sawara cypress, decadent branch, bark
Vessel: Pottery urn
Artist: Chen Hao

This work portrays the autumn in Yangzhou (a city in Jiangsu Province), which, compared with the autumn in northern China, is less cold and more gentle. The summer flowers and autumn flowers are put together. While they contend with each other in beauty, they also show the uniqueness of their own. The variegated orange and yellow colors on the leaves seem to remind the viewer that the summer is soon to give way to the golden autumn.

This work is arranged horizontally in an urn. The thick branches and barks, as well as the big and solid urn, set off the whole work with boldness and power. In the rear of the work are dense Chinese juniper branches and sawara cypress that serve as the background, which, well-coordinated, render the work solid and steady. On the left and right are sacred bamboo and osmanthus branches respectively. They reach out gracefully, striking a perfect balance between tranquility and motion and between density and dispersion. The flowers in the urn are arranged in accordance to the layout of wild flowers in a mountain area to achieve naturalness.

in the study should be concise, elegant, and refined, those in the dining hall can be relaxing and lively, and those in the piano room can be artistically exaggerated. Needless to say, a work should also match the character of the dweller.

Third, the color of a work should match that of the setting. Flower arrangement is a work of art with life, which often requires the background to be simple and unadorned, so as to set off the vitality and beauty of the work. If it is a colored background, then the colors should either be similar or contrastive to each other. If it is a background of multiple colors, the work needs to be single-colored to increase the viewing effect.

Being Coordinated with the Viewing Angle

At an eyelevel position should be placed an upright or slanting work, or a pendent work in a tall vase, or a horizontal work in a short vase.

At an upward position should be placed a pendent work.

At an overlooking position should be placed a horizontal or slanting work, or a floor-type upright or slanting work.

Display and Fresh-Keeping

A work consisting of fresh flowers should not be placed facing direct sunlight, the air-conditioner, draught, oil smoke from the kitchen, or steam from the bathroom, in case the flowers wilt quickly. Effort should be made to water the flowers and change the water in the vase regularly so as to keep the flowers fresh for a longer time.

Dry flowers and artificial flowers should not be placed under direct sunlight or in a humid place, because if so, their color may fade easily or go moldy. To maintain the viewing effect, one can remove the dusts on the flowers with a long-haired brush or a hair dryer set at the cold wind. Artificial flowers, which are mostly made of Terylene, can be washed with soap or washing powder and then rinsed with tap water.

CHAPTER NINE
Examples of Flower Arrangement

Chinese flower arrangement emphasizes the postures and charm of the flowers and branches and the beauty of lines, aiming to create leisurely elegance and ethereal beauty. The viewers could feel the beauty of life and nature through a flower or even a blade of grass. In this chapter, based on the relevant theoretical knowledge and techniques, I will explain the making of the fifteen works of flower arrangement step by step, including the use of floral vessels for different styles of works.

Learning flower arrangement is also a process of constantly accumulating your aesthetic experience. Only when you keep practicing can you become more and more proficient in this field. The following examples are for reference only. You are encouraged to give free reign to your own imagination while drawing on these examples.

Fig. 126 *Spring by the Pond*
Arrangement: Iris, calla, bell flower, Chinese pink, eustoma, leather leaf, asparagus myriocladus
Vessel: Imitation porcelain plastic pot
Artist: Cai Zhongjuan

This work portrays a group of pond-side sceneries. It uses the callas and the leaves and flowers of the iris as the main flowers. The flowers used are few but their colors are graceful and refined, presenting a pleasant spring view.

1. Pure and Noble

A pot of pure white and elegant callas set off by green grasses is a delightful scene in a quiet study. It also helps relieve eye strain.

In this work, a tuft of calamus leaves stand upright, fanning out at the top and concentrated at the bottom. Below are three white callas of various heights, set off poetically by some unevenly arranged calla leaves. Several branches of purple gmelin's sea lavender herbs are dotted in a sea of green and white, small but exquisite. The whole work looks concise and elegant.

Calamus leaves

Calla leaves

Callas

Gmelin's sea lavender herbs

Category: Pot flower
Basic posture: Upright
Arrangement: Calamus leaf, calla, calla leaf, gmelin's sea lavender herb
Vessel: Imitation porcelain flower pot

1 Arrange a tuft of calamus leaves of various heights, which fan out at the top and concentrate at the bottom.

2 Arrange four calla leaves of different heights at the bottom of the calamus leaves. The one on the right side, which is the longer and the tallest of the four, tilts towards the right. The second is arranged at the back left, the third, which is taller than the second, on the left side, and the fourth, which is the shortest, at the front right.

3 The calla, which is the focal flower, is one third of the main branch in height. The three callas need to be different in height and varied in direction.

4 Make the plants in the pot natural looking by covering the flower receptacle with calla leaves clipped into a ring shape.

5 Complete the whole work by arranging a small number of gmelin's sea lavender herbs of various heights around the focal flower.

2. Singing Loud with Craning Necks

The strelitzia resembles a bird singing loud with its neck stretched upward, and because of this it is also known as the Bird of Paradise that symbolizes victory and joy. In this work, the tallest strelitzia serves as the first main branch. Upright and graceful, it determines the upright posture of this work. Other flowers and branches, either upright or slanting, are all shorter than the first main branch. The orange strelitzias match well with the yellow sunflowers, chamomile, and common goldenrod herbs. Although their colors are not necessarily the same, the orange and yellow are similar and harmonious, rendering the whole work vigorous and vibrant.

Category: Basket flower
Basic posture: Upright
Arrangement: Strelitzia, sunflower, chamomile, common goldenrod herb, common aspidistra leaf, asparagus myriocladus
Vessel: Bamboo basket

Strelitzia

Common aspidistra leaves   Sunflowers   Chamomile   Common goldenrod herbs   Asparagus myriocladus

1 Choose a head-up strelitzia as the first main branch, whose length is 1.5 to 2 times that of the sum of the breadth and height of the basket. The second and third branches are arranged at the right back and left front of the first main branch, respectively. The three branches should be upright, varied in height, and slightly spaced. At the bottom of the branches should be an arrangement of some asparagus myriocladus.

2 Choose six common aspidistras leaves of varied lengths and arrange them around the three branches. The longest one extends naturally to the right to gain balance with the basket and it should be in the same direction with the strelitzia so as to echo each other.

3 Arrange two sunflowers as the focal flowers at the place one third of the first main branch in height. The sunflower above looks slightly upward and the one below looks slightly forward.

4 Arrange a small group of yellow chamomile on the right side of the sunflowers as the supplement flowers.

5 Complete the whole work by arranging a small number of common goldenrod herbs around the focal flowers and covering the setting tools at the bottom with some asparagus myriocladus.

3. A Heart-to-Heart Talk beside the Pond

Since the bowl-shaped floral vessel is big at the mouth and small at the bottom, the fixing tools are often placed in the center of the bowl. Flowers are arranged from the central point to the four sides, fanning out at the top and concentrated at the bottom.

This is an upright work arranged in a bowl. The two callas are made more delicate and charming by the two irises. Standing closely looking at each other, they seem to be having a heart-to-heart talk.

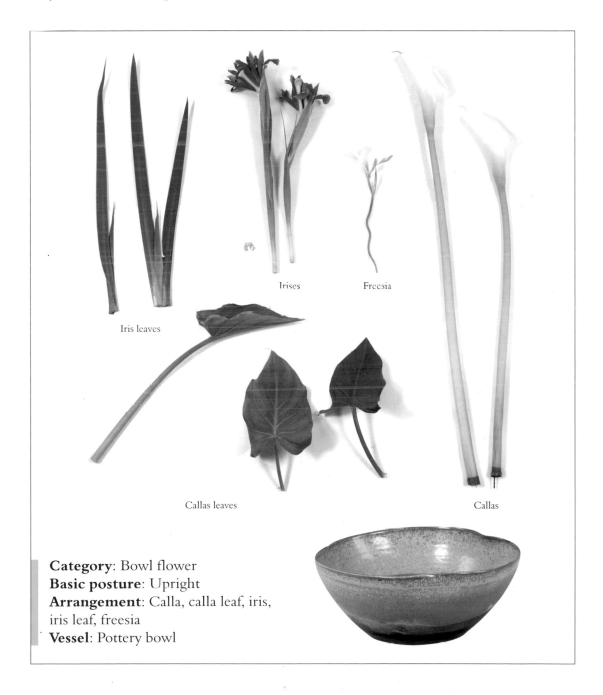

Iris leaves

Irises

Freesia

Callas leaves

Callas

Category: Bowl flower
Basic posture: Upright
Arrangement: Calla, calla leaf, iris, iris leaf, freesia
Vessel: Pottery bowl

1 Choose two tall, straight callas, one taller and the other shorter, and arrange them on the left side.

2 Choose two irises that are about one third of the callas in height and arrange them on the right side of the callas. Arrange a cluster of iris leaves behind the irises. The leaves are about one half of the taller calla in height.

3 Choose four calla leaves. The first leaf, which is close to the iris leaves in length, is arranged on the right side of the irises, extending towards the right. The second leaf, which is shorter than the irises, is arranged on the left side of the irises, extending towards the left. The third leaf, which is nearly vertical and taller than the second leaf, is arranged on the left back of the irises. The fourth leave, which is the shortest, is arranged on the right front of the irises.

4 Complete the work by adding a white freesia beneath the irises, which echoes the callas in color and adds to the agility of the work.

4. Light-Colored Flowers Set Off by Dark-Colored Branches

The main stems of the upright flowers are arranged basically in the center of the vase or on the right or left side of the vase mouth.

The branch of the red-leaf cherry plum is dark in color, forming a dark-colored space from top to bottom with the dark-colored vase and supporting leaves. The focal flowers should be light in color so as to match the dark color perfectly. The callas, though pure white, are set off brightly by other components in the work, bringing into full play the technique of contrast.

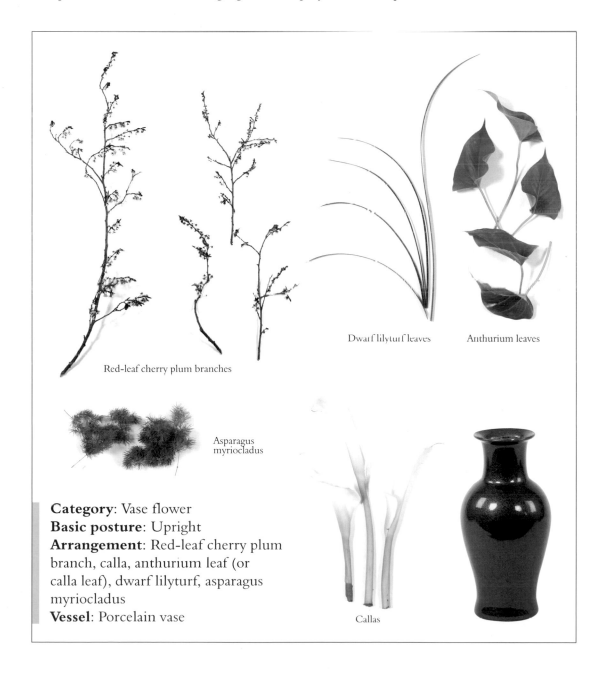

Dwarf lilyturf leaves   Anthurium leaves

Red-leaf cherry plum branches

Asparagus myriocladus

Category: Vase flower
Basic posture: Upright
Arrangement: Red-leaf cherry plum branch, calla, anthurium leaf (or calla leaf), dwarf lilyturf, asparagus myriocladus
Vessel: Porcelain vase

Callas

1 Choose a branch of the red-leaf cherry plum that is basically upright, trim the leaves, and use it as the first main branch, which is 1.5 to 2 times as tall as the sum of the height and breadth of the vase. Arrange it on the right side of the vase, bending towards the center of the vase.

2 Arrange a short-branched red leaf cherry plum on the left side and the right front of the first main branch. Pay attention to the lengths of the branches and the echoing effect they create.

3 Add some shorter branches of the red-leaf cherry plum beneath the three main branches to enrich the frame on the right.

4 Arrange a group of dwarf lilyturf leaves on the left side of the vase to form the left frame.

5 Arrange three callas in the focal area, the tallest of which is about one third of the first main branch in height. The three callas should look natural and varied in height, position, and orientation.

6 Arrange several calla leaves around the callas. In case no calla leaves are found, anthurium leaves, which resemble calla leaves, can also be used.

7 Complete the whole work by arranging a group of asparagus myriocladus at the mouth of the vase to enhance the solidness of the focal area.

5. Egrets Flying in the Morning

In bowl flower arrangement, the plants fan out from the center in asymmetrical balance.

Although this work consists of few flowers, the overall layout shows changes in height, density, and nihility and reality. There is a big space between the two branches of freesias on the right, and the common goldenrod herbs on the left are also appropriately spaced, achieving balance in composition and giving the viewers a sense of transparency as well. The whole work looks like a pair of egrets getting off the ground amid the morning mist, graceful and leisurely.

Category: Bowl flower
Basic posture: Slanting
Arrangement: Freesia, common goldenrod herb, chamomile, asparagus myriocladus
Vessel: Pottery bowl

Asparagus myriocladus

Chamomile

Freesias

Common goldenrob herbs

1 Arrange some asparagus myriocladus in the bowl. Firmly
  insert two bending branches of freesias inside the bowl,
making them slant towards the right. The two flowers fan out
on the top and concentrate at the bottom. The one on the left
is slightly taller than the one on the right.

2 Arrange a tuft of common goldenrod herbs beneath the
  freesias. The herbs are long on the left and short on the
right, so that they gain balance with the freesias.

3 Complete the whole work by arranging one or two light-purple chamomile as the focal flowers, the length of which should be
  about one third of the main branch. This work uses fewer flowers and the frame flowers and supplement flowers have been
integrated into one.

6. Hidden Beauty

The camellia, a deciduous small arbor, is one of the top ten flowers in China. The camellia tree is graceful-looking, leafy, and evergreen. Its leaf, coriaceous, shiny, and water-retentive, is often used in Chinese flower arrangement.

In this work, the camellia branch bends in the same direction as the oval wooden picture frame, rendering itself more graceful. Its green and shiny leaves set off the bright-colored lilies more beautifully. The white chamomile look refreshing and lovely in contrast with other flowers.

Camellia branches

Lilies

Chamomile

Category: Picture frame flower
Basic posture: Slanting
Arrangement: Camellia branch, lily, chamomile
Vessel: Wooden frame

1 Choose a basically upright camellia branch that bends slightly at the top as the first main branch and arrange it on the right side of the picture frame.

2 Choose another camellia branch that is two thirds of the length of the first main branch as the second main branch and arrange it on the right side of the first main branch. The two branches should bend in the same direction.

3 Choose a leafy third camellia branch that is one third of the length of the first main branch, and arrange it on the left side of the first main branch. The three branches constitute the basic frame of the work.

4 Arrange several short camellia branches beneath the three main branches to enrich the frame.

5 Add some more short camellia branches beneath the three main branches to further stabilize the bottom of the frame.

6 Choose three orange lilies, one taller and the other two shorter, as the focal flowers. Pay attention that the direction each of the flowers faces is natural.

7 Complete the whole work by adding some white chamomile of various heights around the focal flowers.

7. Enjoying the Spring Day among Plum Blossoms

With slim branches, changing shapes, and fine leaves, the red-leaf cherry plum is ideal as the material of flower arrangement. Its brown branches and dark-red leaves echo the brown flower basket from afar perfectly. The Chinese pinks, which serve as an extension and reinforcement of the small flowers of the red-leaf cherry plum, are gorgeous yet not vulgar. They surround the focal flowers as supplements to them. The lilies as the focal flowers look dignified and charming, as if smiling in the spring wind.

Category: Basket flower
Basic posture: Slanting
Arrangement: Red-leaf cherry plum branch, lily, Chinese pink, asparagus myriocladus
Vessel: Bamboo basket

Asparagus myriocladus

Red-leaf cherry plum branches   Liles   Chinese pinks

1 The setting tools are placed on the left side of the flower basket. The red-leaf cherry plum branches serve as the material for the frame. The length of the first main branch, which tilts to the right, is 1.5 to 2 times the sum of the width and height of the basket. Arrange a short branch of the red-leaf cherry plum on the right side of the first main branch as the second main branch, which is two thirds of the first main branch in length. The bottom of the second main branch gathers towards that of the first main branch. The third main branch, which tilts towards the left, is arranged on the left side of the basket. It is close to the second main branch in length, but is farther away from the first main branch. The three main branches form a scalene triangle that embraces the flowers in the center.

2 Arrange several short red-leaf cherry plum branches beneath the third main branch to enrich the frame.

3 Choose three lilies as the focal flowers, one taller and the other two shorter. The taller one, which bends in the same direction as the red-leaf cherry plum branch, is arranged on the upper right. The two shorter ones are placed on the left side and in the front. The three lilies, like the three branches of the red-leaf cherry plum, form a scalene triangle, each facing a different direction.

4 Arrange some asparagus myriocladus as adornment.

5 Complete the whole work by arranging some Chinese pinks around the focal flowers.

8. Green Sleeves and Red Scarves

This work is arranged in a bamboo tube with two openings. In the top opening, the flowers are arranged in slanting posture, echoing the lower opening, in which the flowers are arranged in horizontal posture. While the small flowers in the top opening extend to the right and the big flowers to the left, those in the lower opening extends to the left and right respectively, looking harmonious and well-coordinated.

In this work, the dancing snowrose branches resemble the long sleeves worn by women in ancient China and the red flowers their bright red scarves. The whole work looks as if two girls are greeting each other; one is standing upstairs and the other is downstairs.

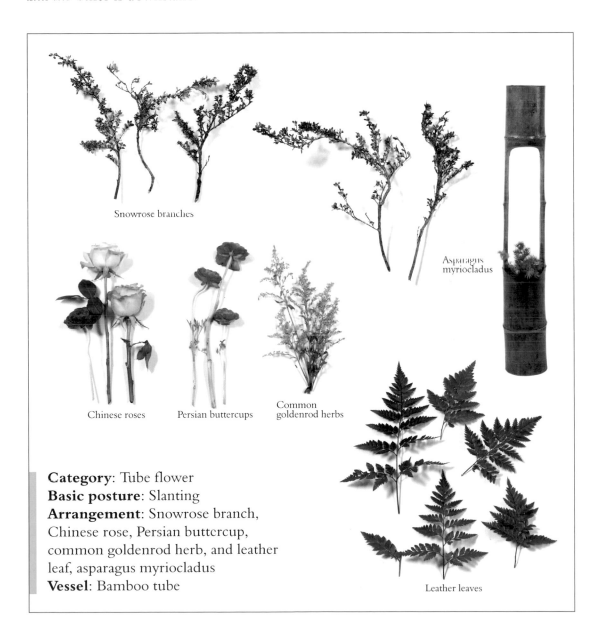

Snowrose branches

Asparagus myriocladus

Chinese roses

Persian buttercups

Common goldenrod herbs

Category: Tube flower
Basic posture: Slanting
Arrangement: Snowrose branch, Chinese rose, Persian buttercup, common goldenrod herb, and leather leaf, asparagus myriocladus
Vessel: Bamboo tube

Leather leaves

1 Start to arrange a cluster of asparagus myriocladus in the lower opening. Choose a bent branch of the snowrose and arrange it in the top opening. The length of the branch is about two thirds of the height of the bamboo tube. Please note that the upright or slanting branch arranged in the top opening normally does not exceed the bamboo tube in height. Second, choose a horizontal branch of the snowrose and arrange it in the lower opening. The branch extends to the left, balancing the branch of the snowrose in the top opening.

2 Add a shorter branch on the right side of the snowrose branch in the top opening. Also, add a shorter branch on the underside of the snowrose branch in the lower opening to enrich the frame.

3 Arrange several leather leaves at the bottom of the snowrose branches both in the top and lower openings, which serve to usher in the focal flowers.

4 Arrange the focal flowers, the Chinese roses, in both openings. The two Chinese roses in the lower opening are light in color but fuller, balancing the dark-colored Chinese rose in the top opening.

5 Add two Persian buttercups in the top opening and one in the lower opening as supplements.

6 Completing the work by adding a cluster of common goldenrod herbs around the focal flowers in both openings as supplements.

9. Drifting into the Sky

The double-opening bamboo tube allows flower arrangement in both openings or in the lower opening alone. In this work, the flowers are arranged in the lower opening. A branch of the false spirea drifts out of the opening and soars into the sky. The two yellow sunflowers are set off by the purple Chinese pinks, forming a vivid contrast in color and overflowing with vigor.

Category: Tube flower
Basic posture: Slanting
Arrangement: False spirea branch, sunflower, Chinese pink, leather leaf
Vessel: Bamboo tube

False spirea branches

Leather leaves

Sunflowers

Chinese pinks

1 Choose a natural-bending false spirea branch as the first main branch, which is about 1.5 times the height of the bamboo tube.

2 Arrange a short false spirea branch on the right side of the first main branch as the second main branch. It bends in the same direction as the first main branch and its length is decided by the number of ramifications on the first main branch. In this work, since the first main branch already has many ramifications on it, the second main branch does not need to be too long, as it mainly serves to enrich the bottom of the first main branch. It should be about one third the length of the first main branch. The two main branches should be concentrated at the bottom.

3 Arrange a cluster of leather leaves at the opening. The one on the left side is longer, extending out of the opening. The ones at the front back and on the right side are slightly shorter. The leather leaves echo the false spirea branches above diagonally. Together, they form the frame of this work.

4 The two sunflowers serve as the focal flowers, which, solid and imposing, form a good contrast with the false spirea branches and leather leaves, which are soft and light. The sunflower on the left is higher and that on the right is lower, balancing with the false spirea branches on the upper right corner. If the sunflowers were arranged high on the right and low on the left, the whole work would have been too weighty on the right and too light on the left, thus throwing off balance.

5 Complete the whole work by adding some purple Chinese pinks around the focal flowers. Since the opening on the bamboo tube is not big, if the setting tool is not conspicuous, there is no need for adornment.

10. Slanting Branches of Purple Magnolia

The purple magnolia was one of the favorite flowers of the ancient Chinese poets. Yuan Zhen (779–831), a Tang poet who loved purple magnolias, once asked Han Yu (768–824), also a well-known scholar, for the flower. He composed a poem of the same title for the latter: "Purple magnolias at the Han's grow magnificently. Could I beg for several branches when they bloom? Don't feel pity at picking some for me as a gift, because if you don't pluck them, the wind will do that for you." Han wrote a poem in response: "The purple magnolias in my house bloom all of a sudden. Do come for some when they are in full blossom."

In this work, a branch of the purple magnolia and the dwarf lilyturf form the frame of this work. The branch does not have too many twigs and leaves on it, nor does it have blossoms at the top. To avoid monotony, we have added two purple callas on the right. The lower part consists of lilies, purple magnolias, and common goldenrod herbs, with luxuriant foliage. The work is spacious on the left and less so on the right. However, due to the skillful use of the flowers, it is visually balanced.

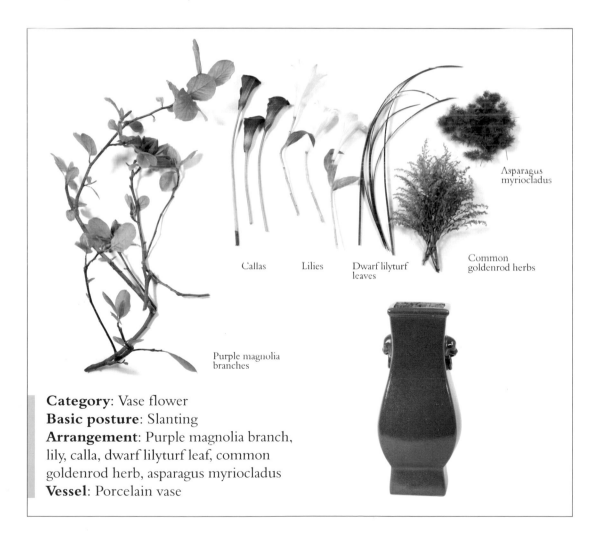

Asparagus myriocladus

Callas   Lilies   Dwarf lilyturf leaves

Common goldenrod herbs

Purple magnolia branches

Category: Vase flower
Basic posture: Slanting
Arrangement: Purple magnolia branch, lily, calla, dwarf lilyturf leaf, common goldenrod herb, asparagus myriocladus
Vessel: Porcelain vase

1 Arrange a branch of purple magnolia slanting on the left side of the vase as the first main branch.

2 Add a short-branched purple magnolia on the left side of the first main branch to form the left frame.

3 Arrange three callas similar in color to the purple magnolia on the right side of the first main branch. The callas are in a slanting position, with their bottom leaning against the purple magnolia branches. The right side of the vase remains vacant.

4 The three white lilies of various heights serve as the focal flowers. One of them is arranged head-up at the back, the second one is placed on the right side, looking to the right, and the third one lies in the middle, facing the front.

5 Arrange a tuft of dwarf lilyturf leaves on the right side of the focal flowers.

6 Add a cluster of asparagus myriocladus at the mouth of the vase to enrich the focal area and produce an embellishing effect.

7 Complete the whole work by arranging a cluster of common goldenrod herbs around the focal flowers.

11. Graceful and Unrestrained

The bamboo tube is slim and transparent. Therefore, flowers that are light and graceful in shape can be chosen to form the frame and blocky flowers can be arranged in the focal area. The flowers should not be too crowded.

In this work, the elegant wisteria branches are used as the frame and the bright-colored lilies as the focal flowers. They work with each other to create a vigorously graceful work. To give the viewers a sense of steadiness, we have arranged the flowers in a way that is light on the top and weighty at the bottom. The yellow lily on the top is contrasted favorably in color and number with those orange ones at the bottom. Despite the slender and graceful branches, the work looks steady and secure as a whole.

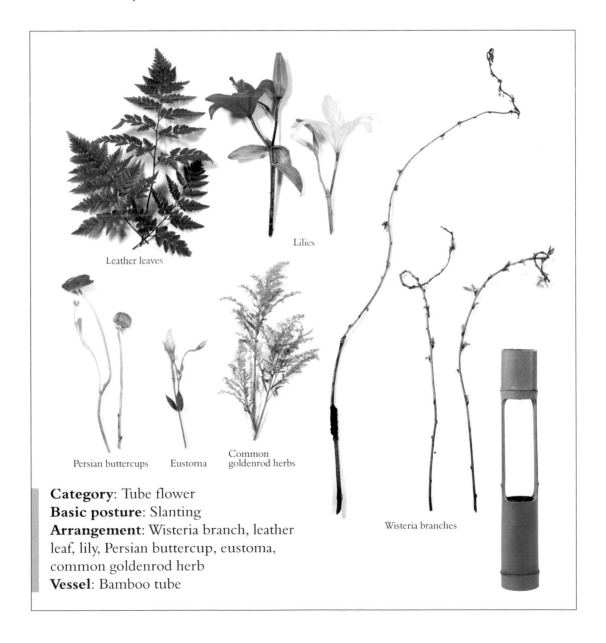

Leather leaves

Lilies

Persian buttercups   Eustoma

Common goldenrod herbs

Wisteria branches

Category: Tube flower
Basic posture: Slanting
Arrangement: Wisteria branch, leather leaf, lily, Persian buttercup, eustoma, common goldenrod herb
Vessel: Bamboo tube

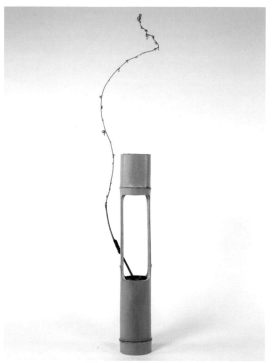

1 Choose a winding wisteria branch as the first main branch. The lower half of the branch is close to the bamboo tube and the upper half slants slightly.

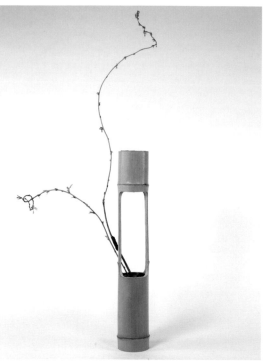

2 Choose another bending wisteria branch as the second main branch, which extends to the left.

3 Arrange a leftward short-branched wisteria between the first and second main branches.

4 Arrange a group of leather leaves at each opening to enrich the frames. The leather leaves at the top bend in the same direction as the wisteria branch, so that they look in harmony.

5 Arrange a yellow lily at the top opening and the orange lilies at the lower opening as the focal flowers.

6 Arrange some eustoma flowers at the top opening and Persian buttercups at the lower opening. Pay attention to the harmony in color.

7 Complete the whole work by adding common goldenrod herbs at both openings. The common goldenrod herb on the right side of the lower opening is slightly longer, bending inside towards the tube and echoing the wisteria and leather leaves above.

12. Conceiving a Grand Horizon in Serenity of Mind

In spring, trees in the garden are turning emerald green and flowers are contending for beauty. I encounter by chance a branch of white-green Chinese flowering crabapple blooming quietly in the warm sunlight. It strikes a chord with me, reminding me of the well-known ancient philosophical lines: "Quiet nourishes one's nature; thriftiness cultivates one's morality. A genuine ambition is derived from simplicity of life, and a grand horizon is conceived in serenity of mind." It is true that only when one has peace of mind and is indifferent to worldly gains can he achieve his far-reaching aspiration. The quiet and elegant Chinese flowering crabapples and the white chrysanthemums are exactly where one can give expression to such a feeling.

This work is typical of flower arrangement by men of letters, who, instead of pursuing ostentation and extravagance, focused their attention on displaying their own refined elegance and taste by arranging simple but elegant flowers in a matching vessel. This work follows the method of natural composition typical in Chinese flower arrangement and resorts to the technique of asymmetrical balance. Long as they are, the branches of the Chinese flowering crabapple on the right are light, with fewer leaves and flowers on them. The chrysanthemums and leather leaves on the left are short, but with luxuriant flowers and leaves. Together, they produce a visually balanced effect.

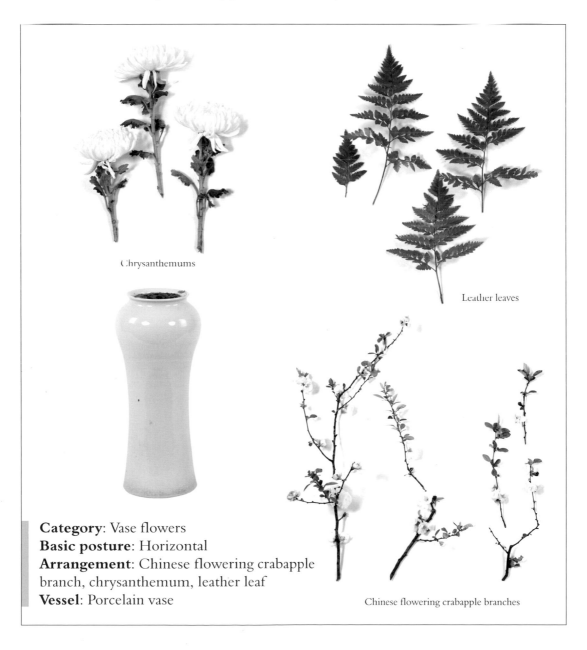

Chrysanthemums

Leather leaves

Category: Vase flowers
Basic posture: Horizontal
Arrangement: Chinese flowering crabapple branch, chrysanthemum, leather leaf
Vessel: Porcelain vase

Chinese flowering crabapple branches

1 A Chinese flowering crabapple branch is used as the first main branch, which is placed horizontally on the right side, with the end turned up.

2 Choose another Chinese flowering crabapple branch (two thirds of the length of the first main branch) and place it on the upper right. The smaller branches recline tightly against the lower part of the first main branch. The two branches gather together at the bottom and fan out at the top, as if growing out of the same root.

3 Place a short-branch Chinese flowering crabapple at the back and on the left side of the two main branches to substantiate the right side frame. The short branches and the long branches bend towards the same direction.

4 Use leather leaves as the frame on the left side. First, choose two longer leather leaves and place them at the top and on the left side. Then choose a shorter leather leaf and place it on the right front.

5 Place a short-branch leather leaf on the right side (i.e. at the back of the first and second main branches) and at the back of the vase to complete the framework.

6 Use three white chrysanthemums in the focal area of the work. Two longer ones are placed on the left side and in the middle, both tilting forward. The third shorter one is placed behind the first two to show hierarchy. Since the Chinese flowering crabapple branches have some small flowers on them, there is no need for other supplementary flowers.

13. Divine Beauty

The peony, which is native to China, is one of the country's top ten flowers. It is regarded as a symbol of earthly happiness and prosperity and was depicted as the reigning beauty and king of flowers by some well-known poets in the Tang Dynasty. It has remained the source of artistic creation even today.

The focal point in this work is the peonies in full bloom; therefore, the two peonies in the center should be large and steady. Another peony that extends to the right should be small or in bud, otherwise the work will look weighty on the right. Here, the blooming peonies and the budding one mix perfectly with each other.

The three peonies, like three beautiful girls, display their undisputed beauty, set off vividly by the branches of the red-leaf cherry plum and green leaves.

Peonies

Asparagus myriocladus

Chinese pinks

Paperplants

Category: Basket flower
Basic posture: Horizontal
Arrangement: Red-leaf cherry plum
branch, peony, peony leaf, Chinese
pink, paperplant, asparagus myriocladus
Vessel: Bamboo basket

Red-leaf cherry plum branches

1 Choose a bending branch of the red-leaf cherry plum as the first main branch and arrange it on the left side of the flower basket. The branch is horizontal, bending upward at the end.

2 Choose another treated branch of the red-leaf cherry plum as the second main branch and arrange it on the upper left side of the basket. The branch leans against the first main branch at the bottom.

3 Arrange two more short branches of the red-leaf cherry plum beneath the two main branches to enrich the left frame.

4 Choose three paperplants of different sizes. One is arranged at the right back, another at the left front, and the smallest one at the right front. They serve as the base of the focal flowers and balance with the basket. Add some asparagus myriocladus and peony leaves in the center of the paperplants.

5 The peonies are arranged in the focal area, the light-colored in the front and the dark-colored in the back, slightly overlapping with each other. Another light-colored peony extends out of the basket to achieve balance.

6 Complete the whole work by arranging some Chinese pinks around the focal flowers and adorning them with peony leaves and asparagus myriocladus.

14. The East Wind Keeping the Roses Company

The tall flower basket resembles a vase, in which a pendent or semi-pendent work can be arranged. In this work, the flower arranger uses Chinese roses as the focal flowers and produce a semi-pendent work.

The Chinese rose blossoms all year around and is gorgeously bright in May. Fragrant and showy, it is known as the "queen of flowers" and ranks among the top ten flowers in China. The Chinese rose was derived from the multi-floral rose through cross-breeding. The fossils of multi-floral rose leaves discovered in recent years in Fushun in China's northeast Liaoning Province are about 15 million years older than those discovered in North America, showing that China is one of the places of origin of the multi-floral rose. The Chinese rose is

often cherished as the symbol of truth, beauty and virtue, representing faithful love, elegance, harmony, auspiciousness, joy, happiness, victory, and glory. It was a favorite topic in many ancient Chinese poems, showing its popularity with the viewer.

In this work, the snow willow branches with pure white blossoms on them are swaying gracefully in the wind. The orange and yellow Chinese roses, which are well-matched in color, are arranged together to create a heartwarming effect. This work depicts a beautiful view of the wind nestling against the flowers.

Category: Basket flower
Basic posture: Semi-pendent
Arrangement: Snow willow branch, Chinese rose, leather leaf, asparagus myriocladus
Vessel: Bamboo basket

Chinese roses

Snow willow branches

Asparagus myriocladus

Leather leaves

1 Choose two pruned snow willow branches. The longer one, which is arranged on the left side of the flower basket in a pendent posture, serves as the first main branch, whose length is about 1.5 to 2 times the sum of the height and breadth of the flower basket. The shorter branch, which is about two thirds of the length of the first main branch, serves as the second main branch, which bends towards the center of the basket at the far end and gathers towards the longer branch on the left side at the bottom.

2 Add a short branch of the snow willow at the lower half of the longer branch to enrich the frame on the left.

3 At the mouth of the basket add a cluster of asparagus myriocladus to usher in the focal flowers.

4 Arrange five leather leaves on the right side of the basket. The one on the right is the longest, which extends to the right. As the third main branch, it is about two thirds of the length of the second main branch. The second leather leaf is placed on the upper left corner of the basket. It is slightly upright and is about half of the length of the second main branch. The other three leather leaves are shorter, arranged respectively on the right back, left front, and right front of the basket. The five leather leaves constitute the right half of the frame of this work, and meanwhile, serve as the background of the focal flowers.

5 Arrange a cluster of Chinese roses in the focal area. The three orange ones in the middle are arranged in a scalene triangle. They are varied in height and face different directions. Because they are dark in color, they also stablize the whole work. The four light-yellow Chinese roses that are different in size serve as the supplment flowers. They mix with the orange Chinese roses to diversify the colors and set off each other.

15. Orioles Chirping on the Branches

A pendent work requires a taller vase. A vase of average height can be used for a semi-pendent work like the following one.

A branch of the rock cotoneaster that bends upward at the far end extends out of the vase, looking extremely smart. The yellow lilies resemble orioles chirping on the branches, filling the air with spring warmth. This work portrays an enchanting scene in a fine spring day.

You could also place this work on a stand, which is then put on a table. This way, the rock cotoneaster branch would naturally hang down.

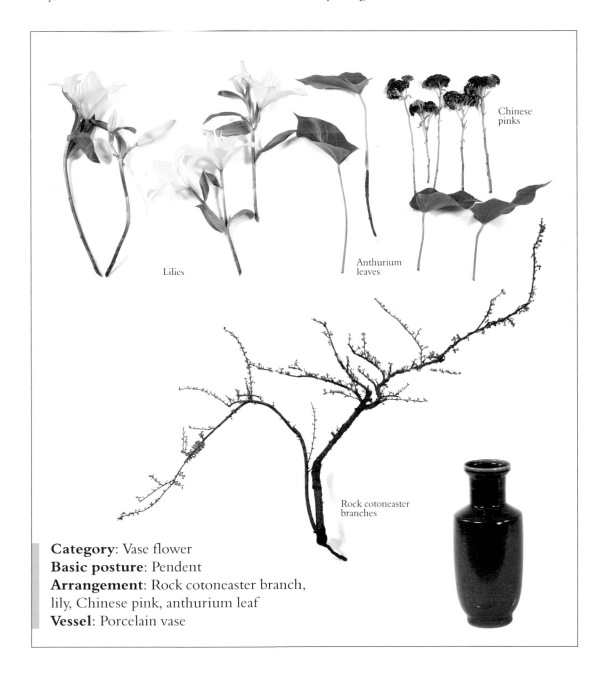

Lilies

Anthurium leaves

Chinese pinks

Rock cotoneaster branches

Category: Vase flower
Basic posture: Pendent
Arrangement: Rock cotoneaster branch, lily, Chinese pink, anthurium leaf
Vessel: Porcelain vase

1 Choose two branches of the rock cotoneaster. The longer one is used as the first main branch, which is arranged on the right side of the vase. The branch is semi-pendent and head-up, and 1.5 times as long as the height and breadth of the vase in total. The shorter branch is used as the second main branch, which is arranged on the upper right corner. It is about two thirds of the length of the first main branch. The two branches gather at the bottom, as if they grew out of the same branch.

2 The yellow lilies serve as the focal flowers. The tallest one bends in the same direction as the frame. The rightward lily buds can be regarded as the transition between the focal flower and the frame.

3 Arrange some more lilies in the focal area. The flowers vary in height and position, and in the directions they face.

4 Add a leaf of anthurium on the right and left sides of the lilies. The leaf on the right bends in the same direction as the rock cotoneaster. The leaf on the left extends left as the third main branch.

5 Complete the whole work by arranging some Chinese pinks around the focal flowers.

Appendices

Bibliography

Cai Zhongjuan, *The Flower Arranger* (Junior and Intermediate), Beijing: China Labor and Social Security Press, 2003.

Cai Zhongjuan, *The Flower Arranger* (Advanced), Beijing: China Labor and Social Security Press, 2007.

China Association of Flower Arrangement Art, *1st Forum on Chinese Flower Arrangement Art*, Beijing: China Forestry Press, 2009.

Huang Yongchuan, *A Study on the History of Chinese Flower Arrangement*, Taibei: Taiwan Historical Museum, 1996.

Wang Guozhong, *Flower Appreciation*, Taibei: Taibei Library, 2003.

Wang Lianying and Qin Kuijie, *The Art of Traditional Chinese Flower Arrangement*, Beijing: China Forestry Press, 2000.

Zhou Wuzhong, *Creation and Appreciation of Works of Flower Arrangement*, Beijing: China Agriculture Press, 1999.

Zhu Yingzhi, *The Art of Flower Arrangement*, Beijing: China Forestry Press, 2003.

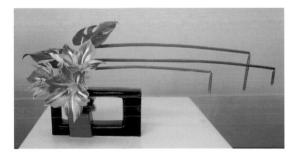

Fig. 128 *Balance*
Arrangement: Scirpus tabernaemontani, ceriman, chamomile, barbados lily, asparagus myriocladus
Vessel: Irregularly-shaped porcelain vessel
Artist: Cai Zhongjuan

This work uses a modern irregularly-shaped vessel as the vessel and is exaggerated and abstract in composition. The three branches of the scirpus tabernaemontani are in an angle of 90 degrees fixed by three gauge 18 iron wires that go through their hollow stems, forming balance in dissymmetry.

Fig. 127 *Vigor and Vitality*
Arrangement: Calla, palm leaf, white willow, chamomile, leather leaf (note: all are imitation flowers)
Vessel: Irregularly-shaped wooden vessel
Artist: Cai Zhongjuan

In this work, the red callas are brilliantly bright while the bleached palm leaves extend to all sides, looking exactly like a group of vigorous youth. The three groups of white willow increase the height as well as the breadth of the work. They are coordinated in proportion with the irregularly-shaped wooden vessel, form a contrast in color with the palm leaves, and enrich the hierarchy of the work.

Dates of the Chinese Dynasties

Xia Dynasty（夏）..2070–1600 BC
Shang Dynasty（商）..1600–1046 BC
Zhou Dynasty（周）..1046–256 BC
    Western Zhou Dynasty（西周）...1046–771 BC
    Eastern Zhou Dynasty（东周）..770–256 BC
        Spring and Autumn Period（春秋）..............................770–476 BC
        Warring States Period（战国）.....................................475–221 BC
Qin Dynasty（秦）..221–206 BC
Han Dynasty（汉）...206 BC–220 AD
    Western Han Dynasty（西汉）..206 BC–25 AD
    Eastern Han Dynasty（东汉）...25–220
Three Kingdoms（三国）..220–280
    Wei（魏）..220–265
    Shu Han（蜀）...221–263
    Wu（吴）...222–280
Jin Dynasty（晋）..265–420
    Western Jin Dynasty（西晋）...265–316
    Eastern Jin Dynasty（东晋）..317–420
Northern and Southern Dynasties（南北朝）...............................420–589
    Southern Dynasties（南朝）...420–589
    Liang Dynasty（梁）..502–557
    Northern Dynasties（北朝）...439–581
Sui Dynasty（隋）..581–618
Tang Dynasty（唐）..618–907
Five Dynasties and Ten Kingdoms（五代十国）............................907–960
    Five Dynasties（五代）..907–960
    Ten Kingdoms（十国）..902–979
Song Dynasty（宋）..960–1279
    Northern Song Dynasty（北宋）..960–1127
    Southern Song Dynasty（南宋）..1127–1279
Liao Dynasty（辽）...916–1125
Jin Dynasty（金）...1115–1234
Xixia Dynasty (or Tangut)（西夏）..1038–1227
Yuan Dynasty（元）..1279–1368
Ming Dynasty（明）..1368–1644
Qing Dynasty（清）..1644–1911

Index